# Collins

# English Through Football

Susan Thomas and Sarah Johnson

Illustrations by Heather Clarke

# Collins

HarperCollins Publishers
77–85 Fulham Palace Road
Hammersmith
London W6 8JB

Previously published in 2010 by North Star ELT
This edition published in 2013 by HarperCollins Publishers

Reprint 10 9 8 7 6 5 4 3 2 1 0

Original work published by MLG Publishing (Miniflashcards Language Games), written by Susan Thomas and Sarah Johnson, illustrated by Heather Clarke

Text and illustrations © MLG Publishing

ISBN 978-0-00-752234-7

Collins® is a registered trademark of HarperCollins Publishers Limited

www.collinselt.com

A catalogue record for this book is available from the British Library

Printed in China by South China Printing Co. Ltd

# Contents

# Unit 1  Introduction

## *English and Football: two global languages!*

Wherever you go in the world, people make a connection through football. Whether it's a group of kids kicking a ball about in a park, or men and women in a high-profile business meeting, football has a special way of bringing people together regardless of age, nationality, race or language.

This book uses the 'the beautiful game' to inspire and stimulate language, conversation and discussion, and exploits it for use in your language classroom. The book covers everyday general English vocabulary and grammar, all within the very popular and motivating theme of football, as well as some basic football terminology for the real fans!

In other words, the purpose of this book is not to teach and practise the language of *football* in English, but to teach and practise the language of *English* in the *context* of football. Learning English should be fun and memorable, and many of your pupils (especially the boys, let's be honest!) will be very motivated to learn English if it has something to do with football.

And, just as football can be played in a glamorous stadium or in a dusty street, the material in this unique resource book can be used anywhere and in any way – whether you have a state-of-the-art classroom with Internet access, or if it's just you, your pupils and their desks.

### About this book

*English Through Football* starts from the language the learners already know, but offers them the chance to do and say much more. It exploits the universally known and popular topic of football, and presents or recycles everyday vocabulary and functions in a context with which many teens and young learners identify.

This book will help you to:

- Produce practical, fun lessons quickly
- Cover everyday vocabulary and regular structures
- Generate enthusiasm amongst even your most reluctant learners
- Make learning English memorable and relevant
- Build students' confidence
- Encourage creative use of language

The units contain lots of general language, allowing familiar vocabulary to be re-used in a football context. There is some football-specific vocabulary and some technical terms (which many pupils will welcome!) where necessary, to achieve the purpose of the activity. You can dip in and out of the units and activities, as with any resource, and adapt them in any way you like.

This book is divided into five sections, and each section contains a wide range of activities to practise and recycle the target language, and these can be adapted across all levels and ages.

1. **Introduction & Activities**
2. **General English through Football**
3. **Football English**
4. **Art & Craft**
5. **Templates**

**nternet: Extra Time ▶**

**Go to www.collinselt.com/football**

At the end of most units, there is also a section called *Internet: Extra Time* whose activities are on the Collins ELT website at www.collinselt.com/football. These activities are tied closely to the language focus of the unit for extra practice, and use other websites or online video clips as their basis. Websites sometimes change (or disappear!), so always check them before you do an activity in class. You'll also find useful football links and extra downloadable, topical activities on the website, too.

# Mini Flashcards Language Games

If you like the ideas and pictures in this book, there are also *Mini Flashcards* topic and verb packs from the original creators of this book, Susan Thomas & Heather Clarke. The card packs are separate with their own teacher's books, and work really well to add to the material in *English Through Football.* For more information visit the Resources for Teachers page on the Collins ELT website.

978-0-00-752236-1

978-0-00-752237-8

978-0-00-752238-5

978-0-00-752239-2

978-1-907584-03-9

978-0-00-752240-8

978-0-00-752241-5

978-0-00-752242-2

978-0-00-752243-9

978-0-00-752245-3

978-0-00-752246-0

978-0-00-752247-7

978-0-00-752235-4

978-0-00-752248-4

978-0-00-752249-1

978-0-00-752250-7

978-0-00-752251-4

978-0-00-752253-8

978-0-00-752269-9

978-0-00-752268-2

# Unit 2  Language Games & Activities

## *Language Games using the Pictures as Mini Flashcards*

In many activities and games in this book you will see that the picture pages can be used as full handouts, as well as home / class-made mini flashcards. Below are some practical activities and games that can be used with the pictures simply as mini flashcards. They can be used on their own or in a variety of combinations to support work at different stages of the teaching syllabus, and with students of differing ages, abilities and language levels. During any one lesson the teacher could also give different pairs or groups different language games or activities or cards, depending on their ability levels and the teaching aims.

The activities and games can be used within any part of a lesson in order to present or consolidate the language being taught at the time, or to develop, re-use or recycle previously taught language. Then, unit by unit, there are topic-specific activities and games to further develop the theme and any extra related language. There is an emphasis on speaking skills throughout.

### Making your picture resources

Photocopy the pictures and cut them up to make (or for your students to make!) mini flashcards which you (or they) stick onto small pieces of card. You can choose whether or not to put the words on the back, or make two collections of cards – sets with words on the back, and sets without. You can even encourage the students to make their own scrapbooks or picture dictionaries with the words and pictures. If you like, you can make large, traditional flashcards for modelling language or for displaying on the board or classroom walls. At the back of the book there are some blank master templates for you or your students to create your own pictures, cards and handouts.

### Dice

The pictures, topics and activities can be enhanced and extended even further with dice for language, numbers, colour, tenses and mood! Visit the Resources for Teachers page on the Collins ELT website for more information and ideas.

### 1 Collect
*Groups of 4.*
Students spread the cards out on the desks, picture side up. The students then take it in turns to choose a card, hold it up for all to see and try to name it. If they name it correctly, they keep the card. If they are wrong, they put the card back. When all the cards have been collected, the player with the most cards is the winner.

### 2 Can you name it?
*Pairwork or group work.*
Students fan out some cards picture side up, for their partner or the next player in the group to choose and name. If s/he is right, they win the card. If they are wrong, the card is put back into the pack. At the end of the activity, the winner is the one with the most cards.

### 3 My Turn
*Pairwork or group work.*
Place the cards in one pile in the middle of the table with the top card picture side up. Students take it in turns to name the item on the top card. If s/he is wrong, the card goes to the bottom of the pack, if s/he is right they keep the card. The winner is the one with the most cards at the end of the game.

### 4 Snap
*Pairwork or group work (groups of 4).*
Students are given two identical sets of topic cards. These should be well shuffled before they play. Both sets of cards should be combined and then shuffled again. All the cards should be dealt to all the students in the pair or group. When it is a student's turn to play, without looking at the card first, s/he takes a card from the top of their cards and puts it in a growing pile in the middle of the desk. If a card played is the same as the previous one, the first person to call out the name of the item wins all the cards in the pile. The winner is the student with the most cards when everyone has played all their cards.

### 5 Guess the Card
*Group work (groups of 4–6).*
Place a small number of cards linked to a particular topic face down in a pile on the desk. Students, in turn, try to say or guess what the next card is. If they are right, the card goes back at the bottom of the pile, but if they are wrong, they get the card. At the end of the game the student with the fewest is the winner.

### 6 Glimpse
*Group work.*
In a group of five, there are two teams of two and one 'games person'. The games person holds up a card for both teams to see but for one second only. The first player to name the item shown wins the card for their team. When the game is over, the team with the most cards wins.

### 7 Guess What's Coming?
*Group work. Players will need themed collections of cards in a bag, box or envelope.*
In a group of five, there are two teams of two and one 'games person'. The games person starts to show the cards, and everyone should try and say what is on the card as quickly as they can. If they are correct and the first to call, they keep the card. After about four / five cards, the games person asks *What's coming next?* and the other players have to each guess what the next card is. The person who guesses correctly gets the card. If nobody guesses correctly the games person keeps the card. At the end of the game, see who has won – it could be one of the players or the games person. Take it in turns to be the games person.
**Variation:** Play the game *My Turn* (above), but if students are wrong, they put the card, picture up, in front of them. At the end of the game, if they still have cards, they try again, in turn, to give the right answer and so get rid of their cards. The player with the most cards is the loser.

## ⑧ Line Solitaire

*Working alone or pairwork.*

This can be useful as an activity for students once they have finished an activity and are waiting for their colleagues to finish. This can also be useful for students of different abilities to play, as the teacher can sort the cards into different levels of difficulty. The student lays out some cards in a line (these can be a mixture of topic cards or just one topic card – it's up to the teacher). The student tries to name the first picture, then turns the card over and checks if they are right. If they get it right, they carry on (with the card picture side down). If they get one wrong, then they try and learn it. Then they turn all the cards back over (picture side up), and start again. The aim is for the student to get a long run of cards without any mistakes. This game could also be played in pairs, groups or teams, where the learning is a shared activity.

## ⑨ Noughts and Crosses

*Pairwork. The learners will need 9 cards.*

In pairs, students lay out the cards (mixed topics or one topic) 3 x 3 on the table. They take it in turns to name an item. When one student is right they turn the card over, or place a coloured counter (or piece of paper) on it. Their partner then takes a turn to name an item. If s/he is correct, the card is turned over and a different coloured counter placed on it. The winner is the first student with three cards in a row, just like noughts and crosses.

## ⑩ I Spy ...

*Pairwork or group work. The learners will need 10 cards or more linked to one topic or mixed topics.*

The students spread the cards out over the table. They decide who is to go first and this person gives the first letter or sound of a card for the other players to find. If someone points to the correct card and names it, they keep it and become the next person to call out the letter / sound. The winner is the player with the most cards at the end.

## ⑪ Kim's Game

*Pairwork or group work.*

Spread out some cards over the table. One player removes a card while the others look away or close their eyes. The others then look at the cards. The first player to name the missing card wins. The card is returned and the game is then played again. The previous winner is then the one who removes a card, while the others look away or close their eyes.

## ⑫ Language Bingo

*Group work or whole class. Choose 20 cards from a topic pack (or a handout from the 1–20 or 21–40 picture grids).*

In groups, one student should be chosen to be the games person. All those playing need to draw a grid on a plain piece of paper with eight boxes in it. Tell the group what the topic is for the game and the 20 words involved. Then they all choose eight words / phrases from the word list and write each of these chosen eight into their grid boxes. From the list or by picking cards, the games person calls out the 20 cards / words in random order but keeps the cards to one side (or marks the list or pictures handout). As the games person calls out the words / phrases, the students have to listen and cross off any words on their grid which they hear. The first student to cross off all eight of their words shouts *Bingo!* This player should tell the games person which words / phrases s/he has crossed out on their grid. The games person checks that each of these has been called out and, if so, declares this player the winner and a new game can be started. The winner of the last game becomes the games person. The game can be shortened by only using 12 pictures and the learners choose eight or even six words / phrases.

## ⑬ Charades

*The learners should be in two teams or groups. They need a pile of cards from a specific topic or a mixture of topics.*

Each team should take it in turns to do the charade / mime in order to win points. The first student from a team takes a card from any pack without anyone else seeing what they have, and then mimes what is on the card for their team. The other team watches and also tries to guess the answer (silently or whispering to each other!). If the charade team correctly guesses the word or phrase then they get a point. If the charade team does not correctly guess the word or phrase, then the other team can guess it. If they guess correctly, then they get the point but, if not, it is then their turn for the next charade. The team with the most points at the end of the playing time is the winning team.

**14 Matching Pairs**

*Pairwork. Students will need two identical sets of picture cards (all 40 or just 20 from two identical packs). You will need to make sure your cards have the words hidden on the back (using small labels, post-it notes, etc. if you are using the colour cards).*

Each pair shuffles the cards and spreads them all out, picture side down on the desk. The first player turns over two cards. If they match, and if the player can name them correctly, s/he keeps them and tries again. If they do not match, or if s/he cannot name them correctly, the cards are turned back down in the same place they came from and the next player tries. The winner is the learner who, at the end of the game, has the most pairs of cards.

**15 I was hungry at the match ...**

*Group work.*

Spread some appropriate cards out on the table (e.g. food, clothes). One student starts a sentence and the next student repeats the sentence from memory and adds an item. If a player can't remember a word, the other(s) can help by prompting him / her with their mini flashcard.
*Example:*
**Learner 1:** *I was hungry at the match, so I bought a burger.*
**Learner 2:** *I was hungry at the match, so I bought a burger and a hot dog.*
**Learner 3:** *I was hungry at the match, so I bought a burger, a hot dog and an ice-cream,* etc.

**16 Guessing Game**

*Pairwork or group work. You will need a set of cards related to the current topic which all the students see before the game starts.*

The first student to play thinks of one of the cards and says something about it by describing it. The other players try to guess which one s/he is thinking of.
*Example: It keeps you dry.* (**Answer:** *umbrella*). *You keep your shorts and trainers in it.* (**Answer:** *sports bag*). The first one to get the right card then takes over and describes another card.

**17 True or False**

*Pairwork, group work or as a whole class with the teacher, or a student, pointing to a picture and saying something about it.*

The other players listen carefully and look at the picture and then the first player to say or shout *true!* or *false!* correctly wins a point. The winner is the student, pair or group with the most points.
**Variation 1:** As above, but the caller repeats the sentence if true, or corrects it if it is false.
**Variation 2:** The teacher, or a student, reads out a list of statements. The players jot down which are true and which are false. Check all the answers at the end.

**18 Definitions**

*Pairwork or group work.*

One student takes a card and tries to define (give an explanation about) what is shown on the card. The other students can see the card. If the definition is correct, the person who defined it keeps the card. Winners are those with the most cards at the end of play.
*Example:* **Goalkeeper** – *The player who can use his hands to stop balls going into the net.*
**Variation 1:** A student produces a definition with some mistakes and the next player has to correct it.
**Variation 2:** A student produces a definition that is completely wrong for the picture and the other students have to try to change what is wrong and give the sentence correctly. One point is given to each player who corrects the wrong sentence.

**19  Beat the Clock!**

*Group work, or as a whole class with the teacher managing.*
Students are given a topic and have 30 seconds to name as many items as possible in that topic (such as *Food, Souvenirs, Transport*), or the names of players or football clubs they know.

**20  Two's Company**

*Pairwork or group work. You will need a set of cards from different topics.*
Shuffle the cards and then divide them into two piles on the desk. Place them face down.
Each player in turn takes one card from each pile and makes up one sentence, which must combine vocabulary ideas from both cards.
**Variation 1:** More piles of different topics could be used, or piles could be arranged so that, for example, one pile contained people, another verbs, another objects, another joining words / phrases, and so on. The players start to play the game with more and more cards to be used together.
**Variation 2:** The students can use the cards in their pair / group to create a story to explain what is happening in the pictures.

**21  Group Sentence Swap**

*Group work. You will need two sets of pictures – a different set for each group.*
Each member of each group writes a sentence on a slip of paper about their pictures. These sentences, as separate sentences on separate pieces of paper, should be mixed up. The groups then swap the cards and sentences with another group. Each group then has to match the sentences with the cards. The first group to finish the matching correctly wins.

**22  Simon Says ...**

*Group work or whole class.*
All the students stand up. The teacher uses the pictures to prompt instructions such as *eat a burger, kick a ball, be the goalkeeper*. If you or the group leader say *Simon says ...*, followed by the instruction, the students have to do it. If you or the group leader give the instructions *without* saying *Simon says ...* first, then students must not do it. If anyone does the the mime they are out, and have to sit down. The winner is the last one standing.

**23  Sounds Like ...**

*This activity is a sorting activity played in groups of 5 or 6. Each group has a topic pack of cards.*
Spread out all the cards, and each player chooses a sound / letter and then tries to collect all the topic cards with that beginning sound / letter. Once all the cards have been taken by members of the team, each member of the team says the words on the card they have collected. The rest of the team then checks to see if the cards collected are right and fit the sound / letter correctly.

**24  Syllables**

*This activity is a sorting activity played in groups of 4. Each group has a topic pack of cards.*
Spread out all the cards, and each player chooses a number of syllables – one, two, three or four – and then tries to collect all the topic cards with words of that number of syllables. Once all the cards have been taken by members of the team, each member of the team says the words on the cards they have collected, and the rest of the team checks to see if the cards collected are correct for the number of syllables.

**25  Spelling Pairs**

*Pairwork.*
Each pair has a number of cards linked to a topic or a mixture of topics the class has covered so far in the year. Each partner takes a card (without letting their partner see what is on the card) and asks their partner to spell the word on the card. If they do so correctly, the 'speller' partner gets the card.

**㉖ I like / don't like …**

*Pairwork or group work. Topic cards are shared between the pair or group.*
Each person turns one of their cards over and says either *I like …* or *I don't like* depending on their choice.
**Example:** *I like chocolate. I don't like chocolate; I like Liverpool but I don't like Manchester United.*

**㉗ Storyboard**

*This activity can be done in groups of 4, and you will need cards of mixed topics. Allow plenty of time for this activity, or allow the students to take part in it over more than one lesson.*
Each student in the group gets three or four cards from a selection of topics (such as *Transport, Verbs, People at the Ground, Injuries*). Each player then writes down a short story using vocabulary or ideas from all the cards. Each player then tells or reads out their story.
**Variation 1:** In groups of three: each student has one card each and one student starts the story, with each player in the group continuing the story depending on what they have on their cards.
**Variation 2:** Students can take their pictures home and for homework they can write out their story, record it and bring in the recording, or create a mime of the story to show their group or classmates.

# Recording and storing vocabulary

Encourage students to keep a record of the new vocabulary they learn. They should always try to contextualise or personalise the vocabulary. Students can keep online or paper vocabulary books, but if you have younger or teenage classes who need more motivation, here are some alternative vocabulary storage ideas:

- **My English scrapbook:** Give each student a booklet where they can write or stick in any new words, newspaper / magazine / web articles they have read in English, wrappers and packaging with English words, adverts with English etc.

- **My graffiti wall:** Stick a large piece of paper on the classroom wall. At the end of each lesson, give a selected student a marker pen and allow him or her to write up new words they have learnt. They should not write these words in a row, but in a graffiti style.

- **My English box:** Students make simple boxes with a slot in the top. Depending on the interests of your students, these can be a post box, a treasure chest, a football locker, piggy banks etc. Students add words. Every two weeks, ask students to open their boxes and make sentences with some of their new words.

- **Word goal:** Draw a large football goal outline on a piece of card and attach it to your classroom wall. Give each of your students a piece of paper in the shape of a football. On this piece of paper, students should write a new word, phrase or structure they have learnt during the week. They should hand their 'footballs' to you.
  Check the footballs. If the words are written correctly, stick the footballs (with sticky-tack) in the 'goal'. However, if you find any with incorrect spelling or grammar, stick these over or outside the goal. Students can then have the opportunity to correct their football so that it can go in the goal.

- **Word washing line:** Bring some string and clothes pegs. Tie the string (the washing line) across the class. Peg out the new words you have learnt that week. These words can only be taken down from the line when your class can use them confidently.

# Football class projects

Some of the units in this book contain project ideas to extend the topics covered in the units. Here are three general project ideas you can use in class:

- **Class football zone:** Keep a football noticeboard in your class. On this, students can post interesting football stories, the latest scores, goal of the month, football photos or a class mini league (based on English tests and scores).

- **Football magazine:** Students make their own football newspaper or magazine – with results and fixtures, interviews with managers and players, match reports, match previews, transfer news, photos and puzzles.

- **Football show:** If you have a digital video camera in your school, spend a lesson making your own football show. You will need to spend time planning this to get the best language value from your time with the camera.

  The show could include filming of a match (perhaps a real school match) with a commentary; interviews with fans, players and managers before a match; interviews with fans, players and managers after a match; an action replay section and so on.

## How about your suggestions? Contact us!

The great thing about these pictures is that the different ways to use them are endless, as you can easily adapt and extend the games and activities in this book, or simply invent your own. Or maybe your students will suggest some! If you want to share these new ideas, we'd love to hear from you.

Write to **collins.elt@harpercollins.co.uk** and we can put your ideas on the website to share with other teachers. Or you can go to the website to see more ideas and what others have done with these resources (**www.collinselt.com/football**). And remember, the website has useful football links and extra downloadable, topical activities, too.

So, now it's time to kick off and teach English through football!

Have fun!

# Unit 3 Football Chants & Websites

## Football chants

Football chants and songs are an integral part of football culture and history. Many of them date back to the club's origins, whereas other chants are based on popular songs and others are spontaneous – they react to an event on the pitch.

Chants are used to support the home team or to slight the opposition. Unfortunately, football chants can contain lots of swearing and 'in' jokes and therefore many are not suitable for classroom use. Here are a few basic chants that you can use. You really need to hear these to understand the tune!

### ❶ Supporters' chants

**1:** *Come on you [team colour or nickname of team]!*

**2:** *We love you [team name],*
*We do!*
*We love you [team name],*
*We do!*
*We love you [team name],*
*We do!*
*Oh [team name] we love you!*

**3:** (Sung to the tune of *Land of Hope and Glory*)
*We all follow the [team name],*
*Over land and sea.*
*We all follow the [team name],*
*On to victory!*

**4:** (Sung to the tune of *Guantanamera*)
*One [player's name],*
*There's only one [player's name],*
*One [player's name],*
*There's only one [player's name].*

**5:** (Sung to the tune of *Go West*)
*Stand up!*
*If you love [team name],*
*Stand up!*
*If you love [team name]!*

### ❷ Supporters' chants

**When the opposition is no longer playing well or winning:**
**6:** *You're not singing,*
*You're not singing,*
*You're not singing anymore!*
*You're not singing anymore!*

**When an opposition player dives or cheats:**

7: *Same old [team name],*
*Always cheating!*
*Same old [team name],*
*Always cheating!*

**When the opposition is losing:**

8: *Who are ya? (ya =you)*
*Who are ya?*

# Useful websites

### General

*www.fifa.com* (World governing football authority)
*www.uefa.com* (European governing football authority)
*www.thefa.com* (England's football governing football authority)
*www.premierleague.com* (Official website for England's Premier League)
*www.cafonline.com* (Official site of African Nations football)

### Football clips

*www.soccerclips.net*
*www1.skysports.com/watch/video/sports/football*

### Football kit and clothes

*www.childrensfootballkit.com*

### Football souvenirs

*www.englandstore.thefa.com* (go to 'gifts' and 'home')
*www.chelseamegastore.com* (go to 'equipment', 'home' and 'gifts')

### Football skills

*www.talkfootball.co.uk*
*http://news.bbc.co.uk/sport1/hi/academy/default.stm*

### Football fans (kids)

*www.chelseafc.com* (go to 'Bridge Kids', then click on 'Fanzone')
*www.arsenal.com/juniorgunners*

### Football diet

*www.footy4kids.co.uk/footballfood.htm*

# Unit 4 Football and Me

PHOTOCOPIABLE English Through Football 978-0-00-752234-7 www.collinselt.com/football/football

# Target Language

## 1 You and the team you play for

**Questions**

**1.** Do you like football?

**2.** Do you play football?

**3.** Where do you play football?

**4.** Who do you play for?

**5.** When do you play football?

**6.** Who do you play with?

**Answers**

Yes, I do.
No, I don't.

Yes, I do.
No, I don't.

I play …
in the park / garden / street.
on local pitches / the beach.
at the sports centre / stadium.

I play for …
[*name of team*] F.C. [*football club*].
a local club / team.
a five-a-side team.
my school team.
I don't play for a team.

I play …
at school / the weekend.
after school / work.
on Mondays / Tuesday evening.

I play with …
my school friends / family.
my work colleagues.
my friends.
other members of my team.

## 2 The team you like

**Questions**

**1.** Which team do you support?

**2.** Why do you like / support this team?

**3.** Which other teams do you like?
**4.** How often do you see your team?

**5.** Where does your team play?

**6.** Do you watch their away games?

**Answers**

I support …
I'm a [*name of team*] fan / supporter.
My favourite team is …

My family are fans.
I like the players.
It's my local club.

I like …
I have a season ticket.
I always watch the home games.
I sometimes watch my team.
I watch my team on television.
I'm an armchair fan!

They play at …
the … stadium.

Yes, I do. / No, I don't.
I sometimes watch them.

### ③ Football team information

| Questions | Answers |
|---|---|
| **1.** What are your team's colours? / What colour does your team wear? | I play in / wear … red / blue / black / white / green / yellow / orange. |
| **2.** What's your team's away strip? | I play in / wear … a red shirt with white shorts and white socks. |
| **3.** What's on your team's badge? | There's a … lion / bear / bird / flower / sword. We don't have a badge. |
| **4.** What's your team's mascot? | It's a … dog / cat / lion / tiger. We don't have a mascot. |
| **5.** What's your team's nickname? | They're called … The Red Devils / The Blues. They don't have a nickname. |
| **6.** What's your team's song? | It's … They don't have a song. |

### ④ Food, weather

| Questions | Answers |
|---|---|
| **1.** What do you eat before you play football? | I have / eat … a banana. pasta. a sandwich. |
| **2.** What do you drink before you play football? | I have / drink … some water. some milk. an energy drink. |
| **3.** What do you eat when you watch football? | I have / eat … a hamburger / sandwich. pizza. chips / crisps. a chocolate bar. I don't eat anything. |
| **4.** What do you drink when you watch football? | I have / drink … tea / coffee / hot chocolate. cola / juice / water. I don't drink anything. |
| **5.** Do you play football when it's very hot / cold? | Yes, I do. No, I don't. |
| **6.** Do you play football when it's foggy / icy? | Yes, I play indoors / outdoors. No, I don't. |

PHOTOCOPIABLE **English Through Football** 978-0-00-752234-7 www.collinselt.com/football

# Using the pictures

## 1 Speaking: Roll it!

**Level:** Beginner to lower intermediate.
**Preparation:** You will need enough six-sided number dice for each group of three to four students. Or you can make a spinner.
**In class:** Put your class into groups and give each group a dice. They look at section 1 and each player must throw the dice. If a student rolls a six, they must read and answer question six from section 1, and so on. After each player has answered a question correctly, they can then move onto the next section.

## 2 Grammar: Tick or cross?

**Level:** Beginner to lower intermediate.
**Preparation:** Make sure you have enough copies of the cards so each student can see a set.
**In class:** Give each student a set of the mini flashcards. They choose two cards and put a tick by one and a cross by another. They show the cards to their partner who makes appropriate sentences.

*Examples:*
**Student A:** [*shows the park picture with a tick*]
**Student B:** *You play football in the park.*
**Student A:** *Yes.* [*shows the food and drink card with a cross*]
**Student B:** *You don't eat or drink anything when you watch football.*

**Variation:** For a simplified version, show students pairs of pictures yourself, one with a tick and one with a cross. Get students to make appropriate sentences about the pictures.

## 3 Personalisation: My Picture

**Level:** Beginner to lower intermediate.
**Preparation:** Bring enough sheets of A4 paper for each student.
**In class:** Ask students to look at the pictures and then give them a piece of A4 paper. They should draw themselves (or stick a photo of themselves) in the middle and draw smaller pictures (or put photos) around to show information about themselves. Give them the section categories above to help (the team you like, football team information, food etc.).
After they have finished, place all of the papers on the board or on the walls. Students can look at all the work, and see what they can find out about their classmates by making statements or asking questions.

*Examples:*
* *You like Real Madrid. Do you like Real Madrid?*
* *You play for your school team. Do you play for your school team?*
* *You eat a banana before you play football. Do you eat bananas before you play football?*
* *You play in the park. Do you play in the park?*

**Variation:** For a simplified version, ask students to bring in a passport-style photo or picture and write a simple profile of themselves on a sticker. These can be used for a class display. Give them the following framework to copy:

| Name: | My favourite team: |
|---|---|
| Age: | I play for: |

2m10

# Target Language

## The player

| | |
|---|---|
| **Name:** | His name's / This is … |
| **Age:** | He's … |
| | about 25 / a teenager / in his twenties / |
| | in his thirties. |
| **Nationality:** | He's … |
| | African / American / Asian / European |
| | Argentinian / Brazilian / Italian / Romanian / |
| | Russian |
| | French / Dutch |
| | German / Greek / Czech |
| | English / Irish / Danish / Spanish / Polish / |
| | Scottish / Swedish / Turkish |
| | Portuguese / Chinese / Japanese. |
| **Country:** | He's from … |
| | Africa / America / Asia / Europe. |
| | Argentina / Brazil / Italy / Romania / Russia / |
| | France / The Netherlands / Germany / Greece / |
| | The Czech Republic / England / Ireland / |
| | Denmark / Spain / Poland / Scotland / Sweden / |
| | Turkey / Portugal / China / Japan. |

## Characteristics

| | |
|---|---|
| **Eyes:** | He's got blue / brown / green / grey eyes. |
| **Hair:** | He's got brown / blond / black / grey / ginger |
| | hair. |
| | He's got no hair / he's bald. |
| **Hair style:** | He's got short / long / curly / straight / |
| | spiky hair. |
| **Face:** | He's got a beard / a moustache / stubble. |
| **Height:** | He's about (two) metres tall. |
| **Weight:** | He's / He weighs (seventy) kilos. |
| **Features:** | He's got a tattoo / scar. |
| **Ability:** | He's athletic / powerful / skilful / fast. |

## Club

| | |
|---|---|
| **Team:** | He plays for … |
| **Position:** | He plays in goal / defence / midfield / attack / |
| | on the wing. |
| | He's a goalkeeper / defender / midfielder / |
| | striker / winger. |

### Family

| | |
|---|---|
| **Marital status:** | He's single / married / divorced. |
| **Children:** | He's got a son / daughter / three children. |
| | He hasn't got any children. |

### Lifestyle

| | |
|---|---|
| **Hobbies:** | He plays golf / tennis / computer games. |
| **Pets:** | He's got a dog / cat / fish. |
| **Car:** | He has / drives a sports car / jeep / 4 by 4. |

### Honours

| | |
|---|---|
| **Club honours:** | He's won the Premier League / Champions League. |
| | He's got (two) cup winners' medals. |
| | He's got (two) player's awards. |
| **International honours:** | He's won the World Cup / European Championship. |
| | He's got (twenty) international caps. / |
| | He's made (twenty) international appearances. |

# Using the pictures

## 1 Speaking: Personal information

| | |
|---|---|
| **Level:** | Intermediate to advanced. |
| **In class:** | Show your students the pictures and elicit the information about the player using some of the target language. Now ask your students to think about how they could complete the information for themselves. Give your students two minutes to do drawings about their own lives. Put students into pairs (ideally pair people who do not know each other very well). The pairs swap drawings. They take it in turns to make guesses about their partner's life. |

*Example for younger learners:*
**Student A:** *You're about one metre 70 tall. You play in goal. You play computer games and you've got a dog.*

*Example for adult learners:*
**Student A:** *Is this a ring? So, you're married. These are two babies, so you've got two children. This one's a girl, so you have one daughter – is that right?*

| | |
|---|---|
| **Extension:** | To follow up, students should research their favourite football player online or in the library, using magazines etc. They should present their findings as a picture, with the player in the middle and with smaller pictures around him. |

## ② Writing: **Star player**

**Level:** Elementary to intermediate.
**Preparation:** Bring in the sports / football sections of magazines and newspapers.
**In class:** Tell students they have to imagine their star football player. Put your students into pairs or groups. They must decide on a name for their star player. They can describe him, using the target language as a model. The pairs or groups can draw their player as they discuss him, or they can cut out the body parts from photos of real players to 'make' their star player. When each pair or group has created their player, they can write sentences about him and introduce him to the rest of the class.

*Example:*
- *This is Beckhaminho.*
- *He is half English and half Brazilian.*
- *He's got brown hair and blue eyes.*
- *He's got a tattoo on his arm.*
- *He is two metres tall.*
- *He's got 100 international caps.*

## ③ Writing: **A guessing game**

**Level:** Intermediate.
**Preparation:** Bring in photos of footballers (ideally famous ones), as many as possible.
**In class:** Put the pictures of the footballers up on the board or round the class. Ask students to choose a player but not to tell anyone who they have chosen. They write sentences about the player using the target language. Tell them that the sentences must not include the player's name: the idea is to describe him for other students to guess who it is.

Now ask students to take it in turns to read their descriptions to their partner (or to their group or to the class). The other students guess which player they are describing. If they do not know the player's name, they can point to the correct player's picture.

*Example:*
**Student A:** *He's in his twenties. He's about two metres tall. He's very fast and skilful. He plays on the wing. I think he's single. He drives a sports car. He's Portuguese.*
**Student B:** *Is it Ronaldo?*

# **Internet: Extra Time** ▶

## Go to www.collinselt.com/football

# Unit 6 Weather

# Target Language

## Describing the weather

1. It's warm / hot.
2. It's cold.
3. It's sunny.
4. It's windy.
5. It's foggy.
6. It's icy.
7. It's raining.
8. It's snowing.
9. It's cloudy.

## Extra vocabulary

- It's boiling / scorching.
- It's chilly / bitter.
- It's clear / bright.
- It's blowing a gale. / There's a hurricane / tornado.

- There's poor visibility.
- It's freezing.
- It's pouring. / There's thunder and lightning.
- It's a blizzard.
- It's overcast / dull.

## Football phrases: Weather

- What's the weather like?
- What's the forecast for the match?

- What are the match conditions?
- Do you think the referee will postpone the match?

# Using the pictures

## 1 Vocabulary: Who is it?

**Level:** Beginner to elementary.

**Preparation:** Photocopy the pictures and make mini flashcards, enough so that you have a weather card for each student.

**In class:** Put nine students into a line in front of the class. Give each student a card. They look at it. They then hold the card in front of them with the picture facing outwards. All students turn away from you. Then call out, *It's cloudy.* The student(s) who have the cloudy card should turn around and face you – showing the card. Keep the game moving quickly.

## ② Vocabulary: **Mime it!**

**Level:** Beginner to elementary.

**Preparation:** Make sure you have enough space in the class to do this activity. If you choose to do this activity in pairs, photocopy the pictures and make mini flashcards, enough for each pair. Use card numbers 1–8 only.

**In class:** Ask students to stand up and come to the space at the front. Say a sentence with a type of weather.

*Example:*
**Teacher:** *The weather at Wembley Stadium's foggy.*
Students mime playing football in foggy weather. Then students say a similar sentence using a different type of weather. They can use the name of their favourite and / or national stadium.

**Variation:** Divide students into pairs. Student A picks a card. S/he must not show Student B. Student A mimes playing football in that weather. Student B guesses the weather. When s/he guesses correctly, Student B picks a card and mimes the weather.

## ③ Listening: **Weather wear**

**Level:** Beginner to elementary.

**Preparation:** Photocopy and ideally enlarge the pictures to make flashcards. Stick them on the walls around the classroom.

**In class:** Tell students they are going to watch a match. Tell them what to take or wear (see 1–6 below). Students run to the correct card(s), saying the weather. (Suggested answers in brackets.)
1. *Take an umbrella.* (card 7)
2. *Wear a scarf.* (card 2, 6, 8)
3. *Take a bottle of water.* (card 1, 3)
4. *Don't forget your sunglasses.* (card 1, 3)
5. *Wear an anorak.* (card 7)
6. *Take some sun cream.* (card 1, 3)

**Extension:** For this activity, each pair will need a set of mini flashcards. Divide students into pairs. Student A is 'Mum' and Student B is going to the match.

*Example:*
**Student B:** *Bye, Mum. See you later!*
**Student A:** *[Takes a card] Wait.*

• *It's raining. Take an umbrella.*
• *It's cold / sunny. Wear a hat.*
• *It's snowing / cold. Wear a scarf.*
• *It's sunny. Don't forget your sunglasses.*
• *It's raining. Wear an anorak.*

**Variation:** For more advanced levels, students should use language for suggestion or advice:
*Example:*
• *Why don't you take an umbrella with you? It's going to rain later.*
• *You ought to take a hat with you. The sun's strong.*
• *You should take a scarf. It's going to get chilly later.*
• *You'd better take an anorak, or you'll get soaked!*

PHOTOCOPIABLE **English Through Football** 978-0-00-752234-7   www.collinselt.com/football

## ④ Listening: **Weather match**

**Level:** Elementary to intermediate.
**Preparation:** Make sure students have a set of all nine weather pictures for groups of three to four students.
**In class:** Say these descriptions to students. Ask students to point to or hold up the correct flashcard(s):

1. *It's 35 degrees. The players need a drink!* (card 1)
2. *The players can't see each other.* (card 5)
3. *The goalkeeper can't see. The sun's in his eyes.* (card 3)
4. *The players are getting sunburn!* (card 1, 3)
5. *Look! The players are all wearing gloves.* (cards 2, 6 and 8)

**Variation:** For intermediate to advanced levels, do the following.
Your star player is complaining. He doesn't like the weather. Read what he says. Ask students to hold up or point to the correct weather card for each sentence. (Suggested answers in brackets.)

*Example:*
1. *I can't play in this! I'm getting soaked!* (card 7)
2. *I can't play in this! It's like an ice rink!* (card 6)
3. *I'm frozen! Can somebody get my gloves, please?* (card 6, 8)
4. *This is ridiculous. It was only a bit misty when we started.* (card 5)
5. *I can't play in this. My hair's getting in my eyes.
   Can you get me a hair band?* (card 4)

## ⑤ Vocabulary builder: **Adjective-weather collocations**

**Level:** Intermediate to upper-intermediate.
**Preparation:** Photocopy and give your students this table.
**In class:** Students tick ✔ the adjectives that can go with the weather words:

|       | heavy | strong | thick | boiling | light | weak | freezing |
|-------|-------|--------|-------|---------|-------|------|----------|
| sun   |       |        |       |         |       |      |          |
| rain  |       |        |       |         |       |      |          |
| snow  |       |        |       |         |       |      |          |
| ice   |       |        |       |         |       |      |          |
| hot   |       |        |       |         |       |      |          |
| cold  |       |        |       |         |       |      |          |
| cloud |       |        |       |         |       |      |          |
| wind  |       |        |       |         |       |      |          |

# Internet: Extra Time ▶

### Go to www.collinselt.com/football

# Target Language

## Verbs

1. to walk / go on foot
2. to go by bus / take the bus / catch the bus
3. to go by coach / take the coach
4. to go by car / drive
5. to go by train / take the train / catch the train
6. to go by bike / ride / cycle
7. to go by taxi / take a taxi / take a cab
8. to go by motorbike
9. to go by plane / take the plane / fly
10. to go by boat / take the ferry
11. to go by tram / take the tram
12. to take / go on the underground / metro / tube / to go by underground / metro / tube

## Football phrases: By car

- There's a **traffic jam**.
- The roads are **busy / congested**.
- It's difficult to **park** at the stadium.
- Can you give me **a lift**?
- I can **pick you up** outside your house.
- We're **low on** petrol. / I need **to get** petrol.

## By public transport

- A **single / return** to…, please.
- The bus / train / coach / plane / tram is **on time**.
- The bus / train / coach / plane / tram is **just coming**.
- The bus / train / coach / plane / tram has **just left**.
- You've **just missed** the bus / train / coach / plane / tram.
- The bus / train / coach / plane / tram is (running) **late**.
- The bus / train / coach / plane / tram is **delayed** by … minutes.
- The train / tube / buses / trams are **packed** on a match day.
- The trains aren't **running** between … and …
- I can **book / hail** a taxi.

# Using the pictures

## 1 Vocabulary: Mime it!

**Level:** This game can be played in pairs, groups or as a class at any level.

**In class:** Ask a student to pick a mini flashcard and keep it a secret. S/he should mime using the transport. The other students must guess the form of transport.

*Example for beginner levels:*
**Student B:** *[Takes a plane card, mimes sitting on a plane]*
**Student A:** *You're on a plane.*
**Student B:** *Yes, I am! Your turn.*

*Examples for pre-intermediate levels (tell students to use the present continuous when guessing):*

- *You're walking to school. Are you walking to school?*
- *You're sitting on a bus / plane / train. Are you sitting on a bus / plane / train?*
- *You're driving a car. Are you driving a car?*
- *You're waiting for a bus / train / tram. Are you waiting for a bus / train / tram?*
- *You're riding a bike. Are you riding a bike?*
- *You're standing on a ferry / bus / train. Are you standing on a ferry / bus / train?*
- *You're getting on a tram / bus / bike. Are you getting on a tram / bus / bike?*

*Examples for upper-intermediate levels (tell students to include adverbs such as fast, slowly, impatiently, badly, dangerously, happily, angrily, carefully):*

- *You're walking slowly to school.*
- *You're waiting impatiently for a bus.*
- *You're driving badly.*
- *You're in a taxi. You're looking at the cab's meter anxiously.*

## ② Grammar: **Transport diary**

**Level:**     Elementary to intermediate.

**Preparation:**    Photocopy the table below or ask students to copy it.

**In class:**    Give each student a table to take home with them. They must tick and make notes about the forms of transport they use during a week. After the week, ask students to bring in their diaries and feedback. You can ask students to do this in pairs. Model and demonstrate the language first.

*Example:*
**Teacher:** *How did you travel on Monday?*
**Student:** *I went by bus and I walked.*
**Teacher:** *Where did you go?*
**Student:** *I went by bus to school and I walked to the shops.*

Now place the 12 mini flashcards on the board. Students should write the names of the people who used that transport next to the pictures. At the end, use the information to find out:

**1.** *Which is the most popular and least popular form of transport?*
**2.** *Why do you think this is?*

## My Transport Diary

|  | Monday | Tuesday | Wednesday | Thursday | Friday | Saturday | Sunday |
|---|---|---|---|---|---|---|---|
| walk |  |  |  |  |  |  |  |
| bus |  |  |  |  |  |  |  |
| coach |  |  |  |  |  |  |  |
| car |  |  |  |  |  |  |  |
| train |  |  |  |  |  |  |  |
| bike |  |  |  |  |  |  |  |
| taxi |  |  |  |  |  |  |  |
| motorbike |  |  |  |  |  |  |  |
| plane |  |  |  |  |  |  |  |
| boat |  |  |  |  |  |  |  |
| tram |  |  |  |  |  |  |  |
| underground |  |  |  |  |  |  |  |

## ③ Speaking: **Transport trumps**

**Level:** Elementary to intermediate.

**Preparation:** Photocopy and cut out a set of transport mini flashcards enough times so there is one set for each pair of students. Write the adjectives (below) on the board.

**In class:** Divide students into pairs. Students shuffle the cards and deal them out, so they have seven cards each. They must not look at their cards. They place their cards face down on the desk so there are two piles of cards. Then one of the students chooses an adjective, e.g. Student A chooses *fast*:

> fast    slow    expensive    safe
> heavy    cheap    dangerous

Next, students turn over their top cards at the same time and compare the types of transport. If Student A turns over the plane card and Student B turns over the car card, then Student A can make this sentence: *The plane is faster than the car.* Student A wins both cards and puts them to the bottom of his pile. Student B now chooses another adjective and both students turn over their cards again. They repeat the game until one of the students has all of the cards.

## ④ Speaking and listening: **Traffic report**

**Level:** This task can be adapted for elementary to advanced levels.

**In class:** Tell your students they are going to a football match, but before they leave, they need to listen to a travel report on the radio. Read out one of the travel reports, depending on your students' level.

***Example for elementary to intermediate levels:***
Students listen for this information:
**1.** *What time is it?*
**2.** *What type of transport has got problems today?*

*This is the travel report on Commercial FM. It's ten o'clock.*
*There are no problems on the roads today. The buses are running on time.*
*There are some delays on the trains.*
*Sarah Johnson, Commercial FM.*

***Example for more advanced levels:***
Students listen for this information:
**1.** *What is the best way to travel to the match?*
**2.** *What is the transport to avoid?*

*This is Commercial FM with a travel report.*
*We've got reports of an accident on the Queen Elizabeth Bridge so the M25 is already congested – avoid the area if you can, or allow extra time for your journey if you're on the road today.*
*Trains and buses are running on time. Due to engineering work there will be no Bakerloo line on the underground today, but tickets are valid on buses.*
*Sarah Johnson, Commercial FM.*

You can find more travel reports online at: **www.bbc.co.uk/travelnews**, or **www.transportdirect.info**

**Extension:** Ask your students to pick out three mini flashcards from the pack. They must write travel reports including the three forms of transport they have on their cards. Students can then take it in turns to be the travel reporter on the radio and read out their reports to the rest of the class. The rest of the class should then make notes.

**Variation:** Students write an email to a friend using the past simple and past continuous, saying what went wrong getting to a match.

*Example:*
*It was a disaster! First, the bus was late, so we missed our train. So we had to get a taxi. The traffic …*

## ⑤ Reading and listening: **Overheard!**

**Level:** Intermediate.

**Preparation:** Photocopy and cut out the pictures to make transport mini flashcards. You need enough for each student.

**In class:** Below are 12 items of functional travel language your students might hear in English-speaking countries when travelling. You can read them out and ask students to hold up the cards that can go with these phrases. (Suggested answers in brackets.)

1. *The sea's rough today.* (card 10)
2. *What's the fare to the stadium?* (card 2, 5, 7, 11, 12)
3. *Fasten your seatbelt, please.* (card 3, 4, 7, 9)
4. *Flight ZA1924 to Cape Town is boarding at Gate eight.* (card 9)
5. *Can I book a cab for Friday morning to the airport, please?* (card 7)
6. *Have you got enough money for petrol?* (card 4, 8)
7. *The 15.00 to London Bridge is departing from platform six.* (card 5)
8. *The Bakerloo line's closed all weekend.* (card 12)
9. *Would you like a lift?* (card 4)
10. *The check-in desks for the Cape Town flight are now open.* (card 9)
11. *I feel seasick.* (card 10)
12. *I've got a puncture.* (card 4, 6, 8)

**Variation:** If you prefer, copy the list of phrases for students to work through in pairs. They can write the card numbers in the appropriate places.

**Extension:** Divide students into pairs. They should choose one of the expressions from the list and make a dialogue. Students can then act out their roleplays to the rest of the class.

## ⑥ Speaking and writing: **Plan your route**

**Level:** Intermediate.

**Preparation:** Bring a large world map to your class and enough mini flashcards for each student.

**In class:** Tell your students that they are going to one of these football tournaments. Ask them to find out which country is hosting it:

**The next World Cup**
**The next European Championship**
**The next African Cup of Nations**

Or, if you prefer, say they are going to one of these famous stadia:

**Camp Nou, Barcelona, Spain**
**Old Trafford, Manchester, England**
**San Siro, Milan, Italy**
**Olympiastadion, Munich, Germany**

**Estadio da Luz, Lisbon, Portugal**
**Maracana Stadium, Rio de Janeiro, Brazil**
**Azteca Stadium, Mexico City, Mexico**

The aim of this activity is to see how the students can get to the country or stadium, using as many different types of transport as possible.
Place a map of the world at the front of the class. Put a pin or sticker on your city / town. Ask a student to take a mini flashcard from you and read it out. S/he must say where they can go by that method of transport.

*Examples:*
**Student A:** [*Takes walk card.*] *I walk to the bus stop in Paulina Street.*
**Student B:** [*Takes bus card.*] *I go by bus to the station.*

Continue until your students arrive at the destination. The aim is to use as many different methods of transport as possible. Mark your location on the map with a pin or sticker as you move.

# Target Language

## Describing the stadium

1. a stadium
2. a car park
3. the ticket office
4. a turnstile
5. stairs / steps
6. a seat
7. the giant screen
8. the snack bar
9. the toilets
10. the club shop
11. the changing room
12. the players' tunnel

## Extra vocabulary

- **first aid room:** This is where the doctors and medical staff work.
- **scoreboard:** This is where you can see how many goals there are.
- **commentary box / media centre:** This is where the reporters and commentators work.
- **VIP (very important person) area:** This is where celebrities, partners and business people go.
- **floodlights:** These are the giant lights for the pitch, for poor light or evening games.
- **security:** This is where the police and the stewards work.
- **dugout:** This is on the side of the pitch. It's where the coach, the manager and the substitutes sit.
- **player warm-up area:** This is where the substitutes run and warm up.

## Football phrases: At the stadium

- Where's the car park / snack bar / ticket office / shop?
- Where are the toilets?
- What entrance do I need for the South Stand?
- Is there a lift?

# Using the pictures

## 1 Listening: Overheard

**Level:** Elementary to intermediate.
**Preparation:** Photocopy the pictures and make mini flashcards. Stick the cards all around the classroom.
**In class:** Students should stand in the centre of the class. Read out one of these sentences. Students go and stand by the correct picture. (Suggested answers in brackets.)

1. *Two bottles of water and a coffee, please.* (card 8)
2. *I'd like one of the shirts, please. Do you have them in a small size?* (card 10)
3. *Where's my locker?* (card 11)
4. *I can't find a space, there are so many cars!* (card 2)
5. *Can I collect my tickets, please?* (card 3)
6. *Look up there, you can see the replay.* (card 7)
7. *Look! The players are coming out now!* (card 12)
8. *Where's the ladies' toilet, please?* (card 9)
9. *I think I'm in Row C, seat number 32.* (card 6)
10. *We're on the top tier. Where's the lift?* (card 5)

**Variation:** Give pairs or groups a set of mini flashcards. Each time you read out a sentence, they should hold up the correct card.

## 2 Speaking: Where am I?

**Level:** Intermediate to advanced.
**In class:** Put your students into pairs or small groups and give each pair a set of mini flashcards (you may wish to leave out card 9). They pick a card and must make a dialogue based in that card.

*Example:*
**Student A:** [Takes card 12] *Can you see the players yet?*
**Student B:** *Yes, they're just coming out of the tunnel.*
**Student A:** *Good, the game will start soon.*
After one minute, blow a whistle and they must pick another card and make a dialogue for that location.

## 3 Vocabulary builder: Places

**Level:** Elementary to intermediate.
**In class:** Ask students to brainstorm and name other places where you can find the following (suggested answers in brackets):

1. *A changing room* (e.g. a clothes shop, a gym, a swimming pool)
2. *A ticket office* (e.g. a station, an airport, a cinema, a theatre)
3. *A car park* (e.g. a supermarket, a shopping centre / mall, an airport, a station)
4. *A giant screen* (e.g. a cinema)
5. *A VIP area* (e.g. a nightclub, a bar, an airport)

# 4 Writing: **Design a stadium**

**Level:**      This task can be adapted for any level.

**In class:**    Ask students to design a new stadium for their town / city. They should draw their design and write notes about it. Make sure they include all the places shown on the mini flashcards.

Give your students these prompts.

- *What is it for? (sport, music, films etc.)*
- *Where is it?*
- *How do you get there?*
- *How big is it? What is its capacity?*
- *What food can you buy there?*
- *How much are the tickets?*

They can complete the task for homework.

**Extension:**  In the following lesson, students can present their stadium to the rest of the class. They can put their designs on the wall for other students to look at. The class can have a vote to see who is the winning architect.


# 5 Speaking: **Ordering a ticket**

**Level:**      Intermediate to advanced.

**Preparation:**  Photocopy the ticket outlines from Unit 40, enough times for each student. Photocopy or copy on the board the dialogue below.

**In class:**    Show your students mini flashcard 3 and elicit the words *ticket office*, *customer* and *ticket seller*.

Divide students into pairs. Place their chairs back to back, so the pairs cannot see each other. Explain that they are going to talk on the phone. One student is the ticket seller and the other is the customer.

Introduce the dialogue, drilling if necessary. When students are comfortable with the dialogue, they can replace the circled words and information with their own ideas.

| | |
|---|---|
| Ticket seller: | *Hello, how can I help?* |
| Customer: | *Hello. I'd like two tickets for the match on Saturday against Liverpool, please. Are there any tickets left?* |
| Ticket seller: | *Yes. We have some tickets in the North Stand.* |
| Customer: | *How much are they?* |
| Ticket seller: | *They are £50 each.* |
| Customer: | *Oh, that's expensive – but it's Liverpool, so OK! What number seats are these?* |
| Ticket seller: | *23A and 23B.* |
| Customer: | *What time is kick-off?* |
| Ticket seller: | *The match starts at 3pm.* |

Students then practise a dialogue like this in pairs, using their own information. The students write the correct new information on their tickets. At the end of their dialogue, they turn around and check to see if they have the same information on the ticket.


# Internet: **Extra Time** ▶

## Go to **www.collinselt.com/football**

# Unit 9  Stadium Plan

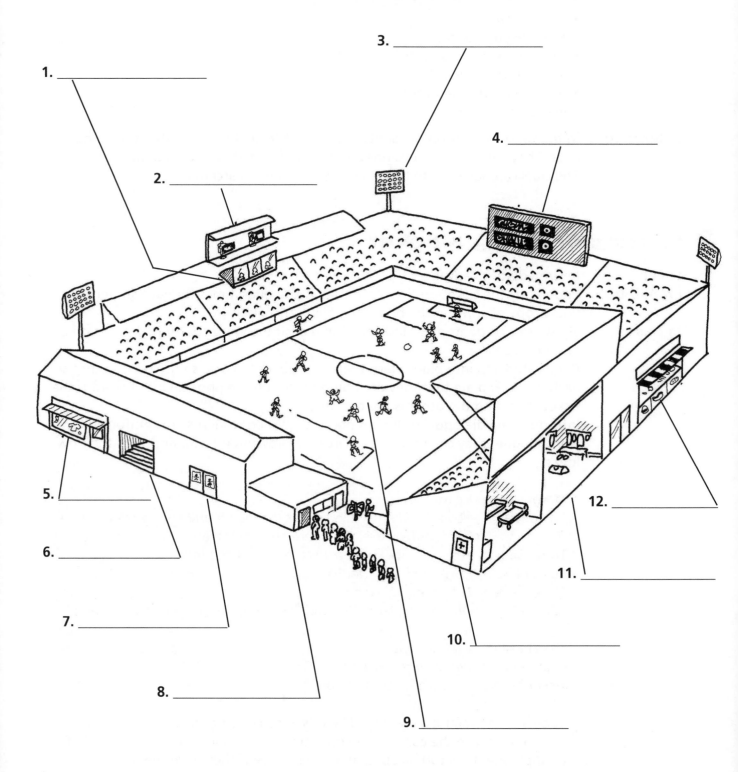

1. _____

2. _____

3. _____

4. _____

5. _____

6. _____

7. _____

8. _____

9. _____

10. _____

11. _____

12. _____

# Target Language

## Places

1. the commentary box
2. cameras
3. a floodlight
4. the scoreboard
5. the club shop
6. (the entrance to) the stand
7. the toilets
8. the ticket office
9. the pitch
10. the first aid room
11. a changing room
12. the snack bar

## Extra vocabulary

- the players' tunnel
- the home / away fans
- the north / south / east / west stand
- season ticket holders

# Using the pictures

## 1 Vocabulary: What is it?

**Level:** Beginner to intermediate.

**In class:** Ask students to look at the picture and label the places using the target language.

## 2 Listening: Where am I?

**Level:** Elementary to intermediate.

**In class:** Read these parts of conversations to your class and ask,
*Which parts of the stadium am I talking about?* (Answers in brackets.)

1. *This grass is too long.* (the pitch)
2. *Have you got a plaster? I've cut my knee!* (the first aid room)
3. *Wow. That's an amazing score. Five-nil to England!* (the scoreboard)
4. *Where's my shirt? It's not in my locker!* (the changing room)
5. *Can I have a large cola and chips, please?* (the snack bar)
6. *One adult and two children, please.* (the ticket office)
7. *How much is this pen?* (the club shop)
8. *There's a big queue for the ladies'.* (the toilets)

## 3 Vocabulary builder: Word halves

**Level:** Elementary to intermediate.

**Preparation:** Photocopy the table below, enough times for students to work in pairs.

**In class:** In a stadium, you can find a *changing room*, *a club shop* and *a ticket office*. Ask students what other words can be used to make compound nouns with these suffixes. They complete the table.

|  | -room | -shop | -office |
|---|---|---|---|
| waiting |  |  |  |
| book |  |  |  |
| head |  |  |  |
| lost property |  |  |  |
| box |  |  |  |

# Internet: Extra Time ▶

## Go to www.collinselt.com/football

# Unit 10 Food: At the Snack Bar

# Target Language

## Snacks

1. a hot dog
2. a hamburger
3. crisps
4. a sandwich
5. a pie
6. chips
7. chocolate
8. sweets
9. an ice cream
10. cola / lemonade
11. coffee
12. tea

## Extra vocabulary

- a small / regular / large coffee / hot chocolate / tea
- a panini / a toasted sandwich
- a jacket potato
- ketchup
- mustard
- mayonnaise (mayo)
- salt
- vinegar
- a serviette / napkin

## Football phrases: Feelings

- I'm hungry / thirsty.
- I'm peckish. (= a little bit hungry)
- I'm starving. (= very hungry)
- I'm parched. (= very thirsty)

## Expressing want

- **I want** a / some …
- **I'd like** a / some …
- **I fancy** a / some …

## Ordering

- **Can I have** a / some …, please?
- **I'd like** a / some …, please.
- **Have you got** a / any …?
- **Where are** the spoons / forks / knives / serviettes / trays?

## Asking for and giving opinions

- **How's your** …?
- **Can I taste / try** some of your …?
- Yum! It's **delicious**!
- Yuk! It's **disgusting**!

## Problems

- Ouch! This pie / hamburger / tea **is hot**! I've burnt my mouth.
- Oh! This pie / hot dog / hamburger **is cold**. It needs heating up.
- Yuk! This pie / milk / hamburger **is off**! (= it's gone bad)
- Sorry, I didn't order this!

# Using the pictures

## 1 Vocabulary: Mime it!

**Level:** Beginner to intermediate.

**Preparation:** Photocopy and cut out the pictures to make enough mini flashcards for your students to have a set each.

**In class:** Divide your class into pairs. Give each pair a set of cards. Student A selects a card and mimes eating or drinking and Student B must guess.

*Example:*
**Student A:** *Is it a hamburger? / Are you eating a hamburger?*
**Student B:** *Yes, it is. / Yes, I am.*

**Extension:** Give students these extra questions to discuss about each food / drink on the cards:
• *Do you like this food / drink?*
• *Do you have this food / drink at football matches?*
• *When do you eat this food / drink?*

## 2 Speaking and listening: At the snack bar

**Level:** Beginner to intermediate.

**Preparation:** Rearrange the classroom so that the desks are in a line. The desks now become your 'snack bar'.

**In class:** Divide your class into two. Half the class work behind the snack bar. Give them all the cards and ask them to sort them out into three categories: drinks, hot food and cold food.
The rest of the class are hungry fans. The fans must come to the 'bar' and ask for something to eat or drink. The people behind the bar listen and then give the customer the card with the correct food or drink on. The fans take their food / drink. Monitor throughout the task, noting any common errors.

**Variation:** For more advanced students, encourage them to ask for 'condiments,' too (ketchup, mustard, vinegar, salt etc.). Tell them that they should use the 'Problems' phrases on page 41 to complain about the food and drink that they have asked for.

## 3 Writing: A new sports snack

**Level:** Elementary to intermediate.

**In class:** Many football teams have their own 'branded' snack bars and foods, for example Manchester United has the 'Red Café' which sells a Manchester United burger. Ask your students to create a new branded snack for their favourite football team. They should write and draw about their new snack.

*Example for elementary level:*
The Inter Milan Ice:
*This is an ice cream for Inter fans! It is blue and black, the colours of our team. The ice cream is mint (blue) with dark chocolate stripes. It is delicious!*

*Example for intermediate level:*
The West 'Ham' burger:
*This is a hamburger for West Ham fans! It is a bread roll, with a beefburger and a piece of ham inside, too. It is delicious with ketchup and mayonnaise, but you will need a serviette!*

# ④ Pronunciation: Stressed out

**Level:** Elementary to intermediate.

**Preparation:** Draw these squares on the board to show word stress patterns:

■    ■ ▪    ■ ▪ ▪    ▪ ▪ ■

Then copy the table below, either on the board or as photocopies.

**In class:** Show students each mini flashcard and get them to say the item(s) on each. See if they can match the words to the correct word stress patterns to complete the table, as in the example.

| Stress | ■ | ■ ▪ | ■ ▪ ▪ | ▪ ▪ ■ |
|---|---|---|---|---|
| hot dog | | ✔ | | |
| hamburger | | | | |
| crisps | | | | |
| sandwich | | | | |
| pie | | | | |
| chips | | | | |
| chocolate | | | | |
| sweets | | | | |
| ice cream | | | | |
| cola | | | | |
| lemonade | | | | |
| tea | | | | |
| coffee | | | | |

**Extension:** Play 'bash the board'. You will need to make two sticks (with rolled up paper or card). Put students into two groups, standing in two lines facing the board. On the board are the four stress patterns. Turn over the first mini flashcard and stick it on the board. The first student in the lines has the paper stick. They must say the word on the card and hit ('bash') the board with their rolled up paper stick to show the correct stress pattern. Their team gets a point if they do this correctly.

# nternet: Extra Time ▶

Go to **www.collinselt.com/football**

PHOTOCOPIABLE   *English Through Football* 978-0-00-752234-7   www.collinselt.com/football                    **Food: At the Snack Bar**   **43**

# Unit 11 Food: Footballer's Diet

PHOTOCOPIABLE   English Through Football 978-0-00-752234-7   www.collinselt.com/football

# Target Language

## Food and drink

1. fruit
2. vegetables
3. a salad
4. steak
5. fish
6. chicken
7. spaghetti
8. cheese
9. bread
10. cereal
11. milk
12. juice

## Extra vocabulary

- an orange, grapes, an apple, bananas, cherries
- carrots, a leek, a cauliflower
- lettuce, a tomato, celery, a radish
- pasta
- hard / soft cheese
- sliced bread / a baguette / a roll
- orange / apple / pineapple juice

## Meals

- breakfast
- lunch
- dinner
- a snack

## Food types

- protein
- carbohydrate
- fat
- vitamins and minerals (vitamins A, B, C, D, E, calcium, iron, zinc, etc.)

## Football phrases: Your food

- What do you eat for breakfast / lunch / dinner?
- I'm hungry / thirsty.
- I'm full.
- I like … / love … / hate … / can't stand …
- What do you eat before / after a match?
- I'm on a diet.
- I'm vegetarian / vegan.
- I'm allergic to … (nuts, wheat, etc.).
- What's in this? / What does this contain?
- This food is healthy / unhealthy.

# Using the pictures

## 1 Vocabulary: Mime it!

**Level:** Beginner to advanced.
**Preparation:** Photocopy and cut out the pictures to make enough mini flashcards for your students to have a set each.
**In class:** Pick a mini flashcard at random and call out an action for students to mime.

*Examples for beginner to intermediate levels:*
**Teacher:** *You're eating some spaghetti.*
- *You're eating a banana.*
- *You're making a sandwich.*
- *You're eating some smelly cheese.*

*Examples for more advanced levels:*
**Teacher:** *You're tucking into some greasy chicken.*
- *You're eating a well-cooked steak – it's tough!*
- *You're smelling some very strong cheese.*
- *You're slicing a leek.*
- *You're eating some very stale bread.*
- *You're drinking some sour milk – it's gone off!*
- *You're eating a whole fish – but it's got bones in it!*

## 2 Speaking: What's in your food?

**Level:** Intermediate to advanced.
**Preparation:** Bring in some food labels which show the nutritional content (protein, sugar, fat etc.) in English. Check any vocabulary they may need help with. Photocopy or copy on the board the questions below.
**In class:** Put students into pairs and give them a set of the mini flashcards each. They should place the cards on the table in front of them. Give the students these questions:

*Which food / drinks:*
1. ... *do you eat every day?*
2. ... *do you only eat / drink cold?*
3. ... *have the most protein?*
4. ... *have the most vitamins?*
5. ... *have the most fat?*
6. ... *have a lot of carbohydrate?*

After they have worked through the questions, feedback the results as a class.
**Extension:** For homework, ask students to collect a wrapper or label from a food they like eating (e.g. a chocolate bar, a cereal packet, pasta etc.) and then write about it. Give them this example:

**What's in my favourite food?**
*Yesterday I ate a Chocotastic bar. I eat a Chocotastic bar on most days. It is delicious, but it is not very healthy. It has got three grams of protein, 11 grams of carbohydrates and nine grams of fat! Now I will eat bananas and not so many Chocotastic bars!*

## ③ Speaking and listening: Food mixer game

**Level:** Beginner to intermediate.

**Preparation:** You will need to lay out a circle of chairs with space in the middle for students to move around. There should be one less chair than there are students in the class. Photocopy the mini flashcards three times. Cut out and shuffle two sets of cards. Cut out the third set of cards and place them face down in the middle of the circle. Make one card to add to this set with *Food mixer!* written on it.

**In class:** Students sit on the chairs with one student standing in the centre of the circle. Give each student sitting on a chair a card.

The student in the centre then takes a picture from the pack of cards in the middle and calls out the word on it, for example, *steak*. The two students who have the steak cards then must swap chairs. As they do this, the student in the middle should try and sit down on one of the chairs. The student without a seat comes to the centre and takes another card. If the student in the middle picks the *Food mixer!* card, everybody must change seats at the same time!

## ④ Writing: Food diary

**Level:** This task can be adapted for any level.

**In class:** Ask your students to keep a food diary. They should write down everything they eat and drink during the course of 24 hours.

*Example for lower levels:*
**7.00am:** *I drink a glass of orange juice and eat some cornflakes with milk.*
**8.00am:** *I drink some hot chocolate.*
**10.15am:** *I feel hungry so I eat two biscuits.*

*Example for more advanced levels:*
**7.00am:** *For breakfast I had a healthy meal of fruit salad with yoghurt and a glass of freshly squeezed orange juice.*
**8.00am:** *I had a hot chocolate in the local café.*
**10.15am:** *I was hungry so I had an unhealthy snack: two bags of crisps. After that, I decided to eat healthy food for the rest of the day!*

## ⑤ Vocabulary builder: Adjective-food collocations

**Level:** Intermediate to advanced.

**Preparation:** Photocopy and give your students this table.

**In class:** Students tick ✔ the adjectives that can go with these food words:

| | strong | crispy | ripe | raw | fresh | stale | sour |
|---|---|---|---|---|---|---|---|
| apple | | | | | | | |
| lemon | | | | | | | |
| steak | | | | | | | |
| fish | | | | | | | |
| cheese | | | | | | | |
| milk | | | | | | | |
| bread | | | | | | | |
| juice | | | | | | | |

## Internet: Extra Time ▶

Go to **www.collinselt.com/football**

# Unit 12 Role-play: Buying a Snack

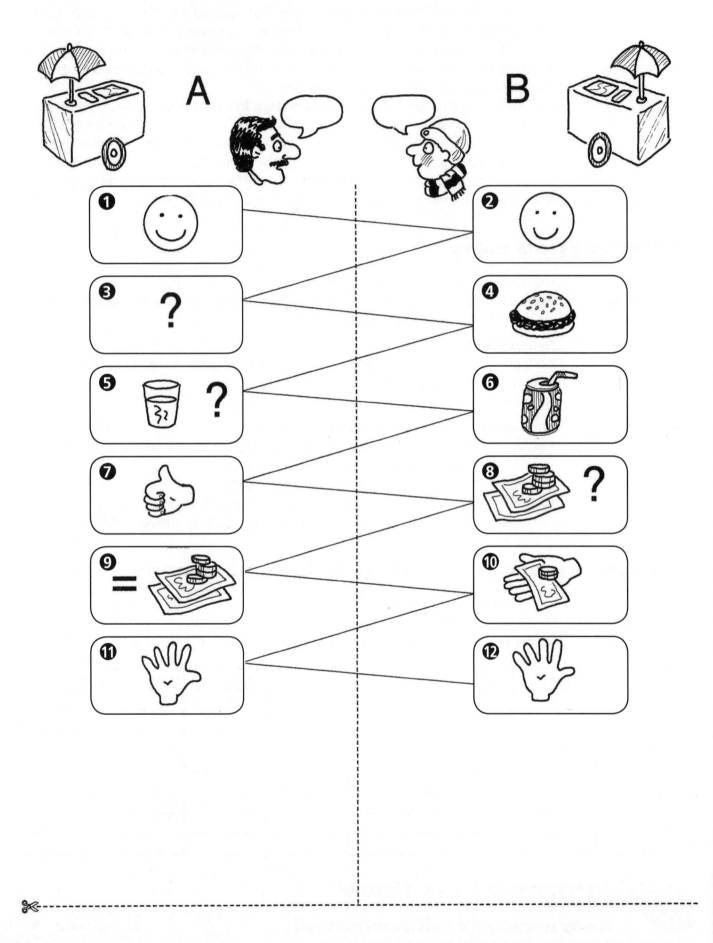

# Target Language

## Buying food

1. Hi / Hello.
2. Hi / Hello.
3. Can I help you?
4. Yes, I'd like a hamburger, please.
5. OK. Anything to drink?
6. A cola, please.
7. Here you are.
8. How much is that, please?
9. It's … pounds, … pence.
10. Here you are.
11. Thank you / Thanks. Goodbye.
12. Thank you. Goodbye.

## Snack bar phrases: The assistant

- Eat in or take away?
- Would you like small, medium (regular) or large?
- The serviettes / forks / knives are over there.
- Your hamburger will be ready in ten minutes.
- Here's your change.

## The customer

- I'm eating in / out. / Take away, please.
- I'd like a small / medium (regular) / large, please.
- Can I have a serviette / fork / knife, please?
- Where are the knives / forks / spoons?
- When will my hamburger be ready?

# Using the pictures

## 1 Speaking: A dialogue

**Level:** Beginner to pre-intermediate.

**Preparation:** Photocopy the page and cut / fold it in half so you have half a dialogue for each student. Draw on the board a snack bar / trolley, a vendor and a football fan (or enlarge the images from the top of the page). Prepare sets of mini flashcards from Unit 10, too. You will need enough sets for pupils to work in pairs.

**In class:** Elicit the names of the characters you have on the board. Start off the dialogue as a whole class, eliciting the language, miming the actions and drilling as you go through it.

Write each stage of the dialogue with your students on the board, before moving on to the next stage until you have the full dialogue. Then gradually remove the copy from the board, until your students can do the dialogue without the prompts.

Once your students have mastered the dialogue, then put your students into A/B pairs and give them their half of the page and the cards from Unit 10. Students should then act out the dialogue in pairs. Student B should pick up two cards and order those snacks / drinks.

## 2 Reading: Sequencing

**Level:** Beginner to pre-intermediate.

**Preparation:** Photocopy the dialogue lines below, so you have a set for each pair.

**In class:** Give your students the photocopies of the dialogue below. Put students in pairs and give them one minute to put the dialogue in order:

| | |
|---|---|
| • Here you are. | _____ |
| • Hello! | _____ |
| • Thank you. Goodbye. | _____ |
| • Can I help you? | _____ |
| • How much is that, please? | _____ |
| • Here you are. | _____ |
| • OK. Anything to drink? | _____ |
| • It's … pounds, … pence. | _____ |
| • A cola, please. | _____ |
| • Yes, I'd like a hamburger, please. | _____ |
| • Thank you. Goodbye. | _____ |
| • Hi. | _____ |

# 3 Reading: **Hide it!**

**Level:** Elementary to intermediate.
**Preparation:** This task is a recycling activity – use this when your students are familiar with the dialogue and functions above. Put the sample dialogue (on page 49) on the board. Prepare a set of mini flashcards from Unit 10, enough for one card per student.
**In class:** Put your students into pairs. Give each person a mini flashcard from Unit 10. The students should not show their card to their partner. Now students re-write the dialogue below, but include the word on their flashcard six times in the dialogue. One of these should be in the correct place, but the other five times are 'hidden' in the wrong place. Here's an example for the card *hamburger* with the incorrect words circled. See if students can find the five incorrect words and check they know which words should go in their place.

> *Example:*
> **A:** *Hi.*
> **B:** *Hamburger*
>
> **A:** *Can I help you?*
> **B:** *Yes, I'd like a hamburger, please.*
>
> **A:** *OK. Anything to drink?*
> **B:** *A hamburger, please.*
>
> **A:** *Here you are.*
> **B:** *How hamburger is that, please?*
>
> **A:** *It's two pounds, please.*
> **B:** *Hamburger you are.*
>
> **A:** *Thank you. Goodbye.*
> **B:** *Hamburger. Goodbye.*

Now students write this dialogue, hiding their own food words in different places.
The pairs swap dialogues. They must find and circle where the 'hidden' words are and underline (or mark in another colour) where the word is in the correct place.

**Extension:** Pairs can then act out their dialogues to the class. The rest of the class put up their hand when they hear the wrong words.

# 4 Art and Craft: **Snack bar menu**

**Level:** Beginner to elementary.
**Preparation:** Collect and bring in some magazine photos of foods and snacks, or clean food wrappers / packaging. Students will also need a large piece of card, coloured pens, glue and scissors.
**In class:** Put your students into small groups and give each group pictures of snack foods, a large piece of card, coloured pens, glue and scissors. They should use the pictures to make a menu for their own café / snack bar. They should group the foods and drinks into categories (for example hot drinks, cold drinks, snacks) and write the price in pounds and pence for each item. They can add their own pictures too by cutting out other photos from magazines etc.

# Unit 13  Souvenirs (1)

PHOTOCOPIABLE   **English Through Football** 978-0-00-752234-7   www.collinselt.com/football

# Target Language

## Souvenirs (1)

1. a poster
2. a (match day) programme
3. a keyring
4. a cap
5. a (signed) football
6. a T-shirt
7. a DVD
8. a scarf
9. a pencil
10. a calendar
11. a trophy / cup
12. a diary

### Extra vocabulary

- a (signed) team photo
- an autograph / signature
- a team waterbottle / wristband

# Using the pictures

## 1 Personalisation: My souvenirs

**Level:** Beginner to intermediate.

**In class:** As you teach the souvenir words on the mini flashcards, ask concept and personalisation questions:

1. *Have you got a poster in your bedroom? What's on it?*
2. *Have you got any programmes? For which matches? What's on the cover?*
3. *Have you got a keyring? What's on it? Can you show it to me?*
4. *Have you got a cap? What colour is it? What's on it? When do you wear it?*
5. *Have you got a signed football? Have you got anyone's autograph? Can you show me your signature?*
6. *What's your favourite T-shirt? What colour is it? Where's it from?*
7. *Have you got any DVDs? What films / TV shows have you got? How many times have you watched your favourite DVD?*
8. *Have you got a scarf? What colour is it? When do you wear it?*
9. *Have you got a pencil? Can you show it to me? What colour is it?*
10. *Have you got a calendar? What's on it? What month is it now? What day is it today?*
11. *Have you ever won a trophy / cup? What for?*
12. *Have you got a diary? What do you use it for? What's the date today?*

**Extension:** For homework, ask your students to bring in a souvenir that they like. At the beginning of the next lesson, ask them to talk about it.

## ② Listening: **Grab it!**

**Level:** Beginner to intermediate.

**Preparation:** Photocopy and cut out the pictures – enlarged if possible. Make a space in the class to do the activity below.

**In class:** Place the mini flashcards in a space on the floor and ask your students to stand around the pictures in a circle. Read out these descriptions. Students should listen and grab / pick up the cards showing the souvenirs you are describing (answers in brackets below). At the end, the student who has the most flashcards is the winner.

1. *I can wear it.* (card 4, 6, 8)
2. *I can watch it.* (card 7)
3. *I can read it.* (card 2, 12)
4. *I can put it on my wall.* (card 1, 10)
5. *I can write in it.* (card 2, 12)
6. *I can keep my keys on it.* (card 3)
7. *I can kick it.* (card 5)
8. *I can write with it.* (card 9)
9. *You can win it.* (card 11)

## ③ Writing: **A present from ...**

**Level:** This can be adapted to any level.

**Preparation:** Bring in small pieces of paper. You will also need a set of the mini flashcards for the class or each group. (You can also use the mini flashcards from Unit 14 if you have pre-taught the vocabulary.)

**In class:** Students can work as a class or in groups. Tell your students to choose a mini flashcard. Hand out the small pieces of paper and ask the students to write their name on one side and to fold it so their name cannot be seen. Collect the paper and then hand it out to each student, making sure they do not have the piece of paper with their own name on it. The student should then write a short message on the back of the flashcard, then 'give' their souvenir flashcard to the person whose name they have. Give them a language model on the board.

*Example for beginner level:*
*To ...*
*Here is your present. It is a Manchester United keyring.*
*Love from ...*

*Example for intermediate level:*
*Dear ...*
*I went to the World Cup. It was fantastic! Here is a souvenir for you. It is a World Cup T-shirt. I hope you like it!*
*Love from ...*

*Example for advanced level:*
*Dear ...*
*I am back from my trip to the World Cup! I am enclosing your souvenir all the way from South Africa. It is a World Cup DVD! I am sure you will treasure it forever!*
*Love from ...*

**Extension:** The receiver of the 'gift' should then write or email back a thank you letter. Give them a language model on the board.

*Example for beginner level:*
*Dear …*
*Thank you for the keyring. I love it!*
*From …*

*Example for intermediate level:*
*Dear …*
*Thank you for bringing me a souvenir from the World Cup. I love the T-shirt and I can't wait to wear it!*
*Love …*

*Example for advanced level:*
*Dear …*
*Thank you for the fantastic DVD you bought me all the way back from South Africa. It is really thoughtful of you. I look forward to watching it!*
*Love from …*

**Variation:** Encourage advanced students to be more creative with their exchanges. They can pretend the present is inappropriate – maybe they don't like football or the club the souvenir is from – would you give a Real Madrid fan a Barcelona shirt, for example?

## 4 Vocabulary: Pass the ball!

**Level:** Intermediate to advanced.

**Preparation:** Photocopy the football outline from Unit 35 enough times for your students to work in groups of four. If you have one, bring a whistle to their class. Draw a goal on your classroom board (make sure you have some adhesive close to the board).

**In class:** Put your students into teams of four and ask each team to sit in a circle. They should each have a pen. Place the photocopy of the football in the middle of each team's circle.

Give each team a flashcard. The idea is for each team to write as many words as possible in the same lexical set as the card. So for example if the team has card 6 showing the shirt, the must write as many words as possible related to clothes. As you give out the cards, state the name of the lexical set you want them to practise and blow a whistle. One person in the team writes a word in that category in one of the white spaces on the football. S/he then passes the football to their left to the next team member who must write a different word in that lexical set in another white space. S/he then passes the football to the left again and the next person writes another word and so on. When the white spaces are full or they cannot think of any more words, they take their football to the board and stick it in the goal. They score a goal if all the words are spelt correctly.

**Extension:** You can repeat the game with other lexical sets.

## Internet: Extra Time ▶

**Go to www.collinselt.com/football**

# Unit 14 Souvenirs (2)

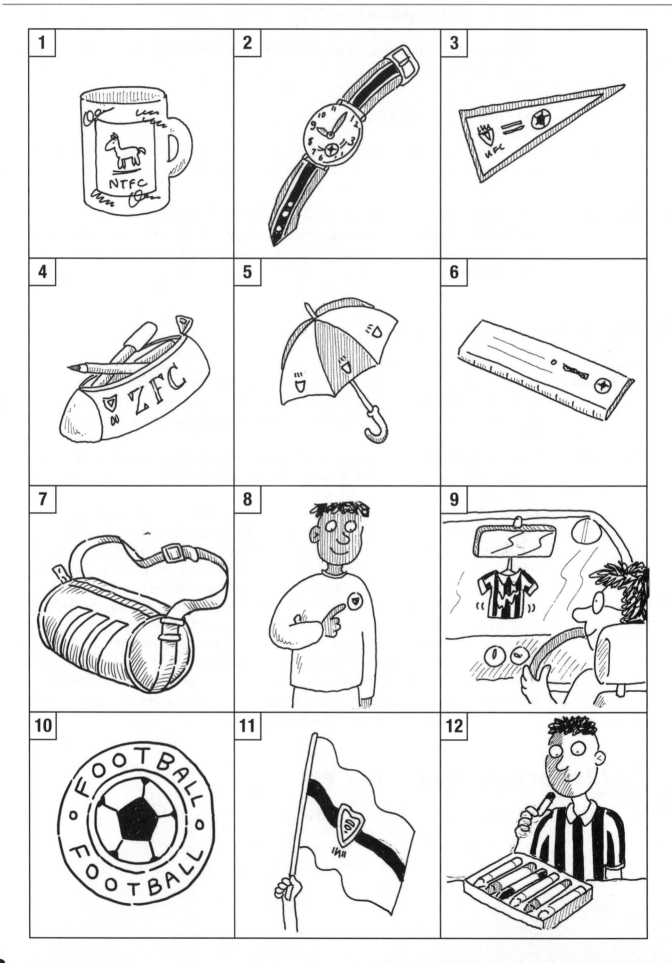

# Target Language

## At the club shop

1. a mug
2. a watch
3. a pennant
4. a pencil case
5. an umbrella
6. a ruler
7. a sports bag
8. a badge / pin
9. a car kit
10. a car sticker
11. a flag
12. face paints

## Shopping phrases: The customer

- Excuse me, can you help me?
- I'm looking for a …
- Have you got any … / Have you got anything suitable for a …?
- Have you got anything under (ten) pounds?
- Can I get my name printed on this shirt / mug?

## The assistant

- We've got these … They're on special offer.
- How / What about this fantastic / lovely / beautiful …?
- I'd suggest …

# Using the pictures

## 1 Personalisation: My souvenirs

**Level:** Beginner to intermediate.

**In class:** Ask these concept and personalisation questions as you hold up and say the word(s) for each mini flashcard:

1. *Have you got a mug? What's on it? What's your favourite hot drink?*
2. *Have you got a watch? What colour is it? Is it digital? Who gave it to you? What time is it now?*
3. *Where do you see pennants?*
4. *Can you show me your pencil case? What's in it? What colour is it?*
5. *When do you use an umbrella? Have you got an umbrella? What colour is it?*
6. *What can you use a ruler for?*
7. *Have you got a sports bag? What do you carry in it? What colour is it? What make is it?*
8. *Do you wear badges? What's on them?*
9. *Do your parents have a car?*
10. *Is there a car sticker on it? What car stickers do you see?*
11. *What is on our national flag?*
12. *Have you ever painted your face? What colour? When?*

## 2 Vocabulary: Mime it!

**Level:** Beginner to pre-intermediate.
**Preparation:** Photocopy and cut out the pictures to make enough mini flashcards for your students to have a set each.
**In class:** Divide your class into pairs. They should each take turns to pick a card and mime how they would use the souvenir. The other student should guess the souvenir.

*Example:*
**Student A:** [*mimes putting up an umbrella*]
**Student B:** *Have you got an umbrella?*

## 3 Listening: Grab it!

**Level:** Beginner to intermediate.
**Preparation:** Photocopy and cut out the pictures from both Unit 13 and Unit 14 – enlarged if possible. Make a space in the class to do the activity below.
**In class:** Place the mini flashcards in a space on the floor and ask your students to stand around the pictures in a circle. Read out these descriptions of people. Students should listen and grab / pick up the cards which would make good presents for these people (suggested answers in brackets below).
At the end, the student who has the most flashcards is the winner.

1. *This person owns a car.* (card 9, 10 and card 3 from Unit 13)
2. *This person is always late.* (card 2, maybe card 10 from Unit 13)
3. *This person is at school.* (card 4, 6, 7 and card 9 from Unit 13)
4. *This person lives in a rainy country.* (card 5, maybe card 4 from Unit 13)
5. *This person loves coffee.* (card 1)

## 4 Speaking: In the shop

**Level:** Intermediate to advanced.
**In class:** First review the shopping phrases on page 57. Then divide the class into pairs. Give each pair of students a set of mini flashcards with all the souvenirs. Then ask them to act out a scene in a shop.
Student A is the customer looking for a present and Student B is the helpful sales assistant.

*Example:*
**Student A:** *Excuse me, could you help me? I'm looking for a present for my fourteen-year-old cousin.*
**Student B:** *We've got this watch. It's got the team colours on it.*
**Student A:** *Have you got anything under five pounds?*
**Student B:** *We've got these fantastic car stickers. They're on special offer.*

**Variation:** Encourage students to include items that are not on the flashcards to extend their dialogue. Get some of the pairs to act out their dialogues to the class.

## 5 Writing and speaking: Who's it for?

**Level:** Intermediate to advanced.
**In class:** First, ask students to write down a list of five to ten people they know. Encourage them to think of people of different ages.
Now ask them to look at the flashcards of the souvenirs. Their task is to match at least one souvenir with the people on their list. They must think about why that souvenir is most suitable for that person.

PHOTOCOPIABLE **English Through Football** 978-0-00-752234-7   www.collinselt.com/football

When they have finished, they discuss their choices with a partner.

*Example:*
**Student A:** *This is my grandfather. I've chosen the car sticker for him because he loves driving.*
**Student B:** *This is my friend Alison. I've chosen the face paints for her because she loves to look interesting and different.*

## 6 Writing: Football emblems

**Level:** This task can be adapted to any level.

**Preparation:** Bring in some examples of famous football emblems and badges to class. Photocopy the emblem from Unit 36 enough times for each student to have a copy.

**In class:** Explain to your students that most football teams (and some families) have their own emblems. Show your students examples of different football emblems and badges and point out how these are often made up of different symbols that represent the team (or family).

Ask students to design their own emblem. Give students the emblem outline from Unit 36. Students draw an emblem to represent four aspect of themselves (family, lifestyle, hometown etc.).

When students have finished, they can talk about their emblem to the class, or you could display their work on the classroom wall and ask other classmates to identify who the person is.

**Variation:** Students draw a new emblem to represent their favourite team.

# Unit 15 Football Kit

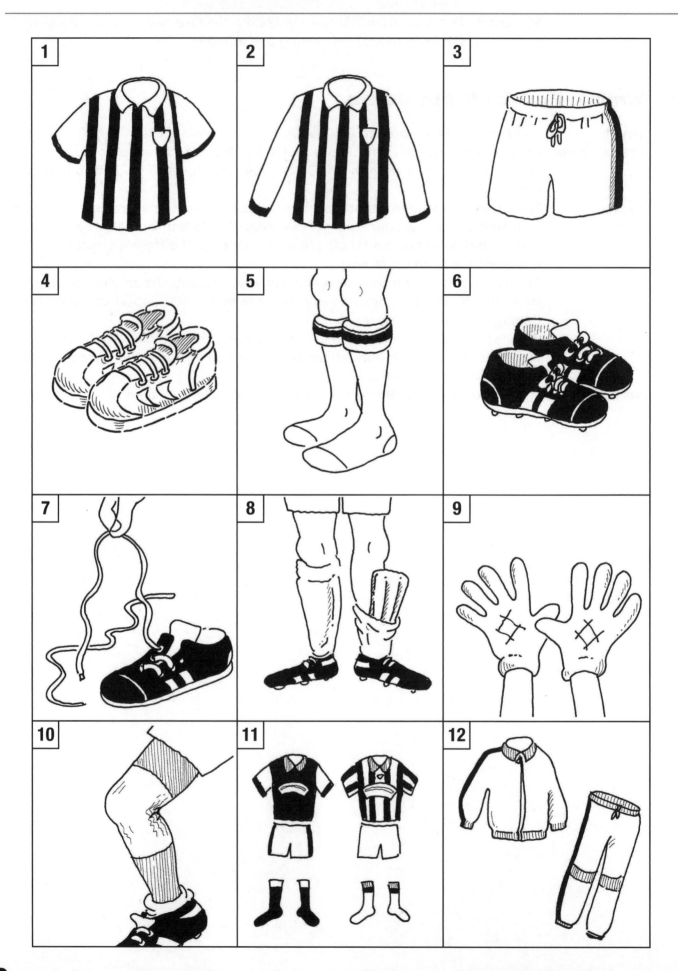

# Target Language

## Clothes

1. a (short-sleeved) football shirt
2. a (long-sleeved) football shirt
3. shorts
4. trainers
5. socks
6. football boots
7. laces
8. shinpads / shinguards
9. gloves
10. a support bandage
11. a home / away kit
12. a tracksuit

## Extra vocabulary: Materials

- to be made of cotton / wool / leather / man-made material / synthetics
- lightweight

## Patterns and logos

- plain
- (horizontal / vertical) stripes
- a stripy / striped / spotty shirt

- spots / diamonds
- the shirt sponsor is …
- the emblem is …

## Appearance

- clean
- dirty

- muddy
- grass-stained

# Using the pictures

## 1 Vocabulary: Mime it!

**Level:** Beginner to intermediate.

**In class:** Present the words using the mini flashcards. Then ask your students to stand in a space in the classroom. Call out instructions and they should mime the actions.

*Examples for beginner to intermediate level:*
- *Put on your football shirt.*
- *Put on your shorts.*
- *Put on your gloves.*
- *Put on your socks.*
- *Put on your trainers.*

*Examples for intermediate level:*
- *Tie up your laces.*
- *Wash your socks.*
- *Iron your shirt.*
- *Take off your boots.*
- *Clean your muddy boots.*
- *Hang your clothes on the washing line.*

**Extension:** Divide your class into pairs, and give each pair a set of mini flashcards. One student takes a card and gives an instruction for the others to mime. They can then swap roles.

## 2 Vocabulary: The washing line game

**Level:** Beginner to elementary. This activity works best in smaller classes and with younger learners.

**Preparation:** Before the lesson, photocopy and cut out the pictures to make mini flashcards (you can use the pictures from Unit 16 if students have learnt these, too). Place some string across the board in the style of a washing line. Attach all the pictures to your washing line with clothes pegs or paper clips. The pictures should be facing towards the board, so your students cannot see the pictures.

**In class:** Divide the class into two teams. One team starts. Take a card from one end of the line and turn over the picture so the first team can see it. A student from the team must say or write the word in English – if they are correct, their team can move onto the next card from the line. If they are wrong, the other team gets a turn. They must start back at the beginning of the line. The aim is to name all the cards in order from one end of the line to the other.

**Extension:** To follow up, students can create their own washing lines, using string, paper to draw the clothes and paperclips for clothes pegs.

## 3 Vocabulary: Clothes grab

**Level:** Beginner to intermediate.

**In class:** Divide your class into two halves so you have two teams of equal numbers. The two teams stand in a line facing each other with a gap in between them. Put a set of mini flashcards face up in a line in the gap between the teams. Give each member of each team a letter, so you have two As, two Bs etc. Then call out one of the letters, then an item of clothing. The two students with that letter must run and pick up / grab the correct mini flashcard. Continue with another letter and another item of clothing. At the end, the team who has the most kit cards wins.

## 4 Speaking: **Discussion**

**Level:**           Intermediate.
**Preparation:**     Before the lesson, photocopy the questions below or copy them onto the board.
**In class:**        Put students into pairs and ask them to discuss these questions. Give them a time limit, then feedback as a class and discuss your students' answers.

1. *Describe your national team's football kit. What colours do they play in? Why? What is the emblem on the shirt? What does it mean?*
2. *Describe your favourite football team's kit.*
3. *Does your team have a sponsor? Who is it? Why do teams have sponsors?*
4. *How often does your team change its kit? Why do you think teams change their kits so often?*
5. *What colours are best for a football kit? Why? Are there any colours which are not good? Why?*

## 5 Writing: **Design a kit**

**Level:**           This task can be adapted for any level.
**Preparation:**     Before the lesson, photocopy the outline of a football kit from Unit 37.
**In class:**        Give your students the outlines of a kit. Ask them to design a new kit for their favourite team or their national team and write a description of the kit. Students should present their kits to the class and have a vote to see which is the most popular.

*Example for beginner to intermediate level:*
**My new kit**
*This is a new football kit for …*
*The shirt is blue and white.*
*The tracksuit is made of cotton.*

*Example for advanced levels:*
**My new kit**
*The new kit for my team will be lightweight and made of a special man-made material to prevent the player from too getting hot or too cold. It will also dry quickly in wet weather and will not show any mud or grass stains.*

## 6 Vocabulary: **Beetle game**

**Level:**           Pre-intermediate to advanced.
**Preparation:**     Bring enough dice for your students to have one for groups of three to four. Photocopy the Football Kit: Beetle Game from Unit 38 enough times for each student in your class. Cut up the cards.
**In class:**        Divide your class into small groups. Give each group a dice and a set of Beetle game cards each. Spread the cards out over the table. Students take turns to throw the dice. They then ask for the item of kit for that number.

*Example: I've got number 5. Can I have a sock please?*

The player with the sock card must give the student the correct card. Then the next player throws the dice and so on. The winner is the player who gets the complete 'beetle' i.e. the complete kit.

# Unit 16 Football Clothes & Accessories

PHOTOCOPIABLE   English Through Football 978-0-00-752234-7   www.collinselt.com/football

# Target Language

## Clothes and accessories

1. a baseball cap
2. a beanie hat
3. a scarf
4. (a pair of) trainers
5. a sweater / jumper
6. a T-shirt
7. a shirt
8. a tie
9. a blazer
10. (a pair of) trousers
11. a sports / kit bag
12. a rucksack

## Football phrases: The customer

- I'm looking for a / a pair of …
- Have you got any … in red / blue / green / pink / grey?
- I'm a size …
- I'm small / medium / large.
- Can I try this / them on?
- Where's the fitting / changing room?
- Sorry, it's / they're too big / small / short / tight / long.

## The shop assistant

- Can I help you?
- What size are you?
- Try this.

- Sorry, we haven't got any in your size.
- Sorry, we're out of stock.
- Try another branch. / You can order online.

# Using the pictures

## 1 Personalisation: My clothes and accessories

**Level:** Beginner to elementary.

**In class:** As you teach the items, ask concept and personalisation questions:

1. *Have you got baseball cap? What colour is it? What's on the front?*
2. *Have you got a beanie hat? Which famous people wear beanie hats?*
3. *When do you wear a scarf? What colour's your scarf?*
4. *How many pairs of trainers have you got? What famous brands of trainers do you know? When do you wear trainers?*
5. *How many students are wearing jumpers in this class?*
6. *How many people are wearing T-Shirts in this class?*
7. *How many shirts have you got? Can you iron a shirt?*
8. *When do you wear a tie? Can you tie a tie?*
9. *Where do people wear blazers?*
10. *What colour are your trousers?*
11. *What's in your sports bag?*
12. *On which part of your body do you carry a rucksack?*

## ② Vocabulary: **Back to the board**

**Level:** Elementary to intermediate.

**Preparation:** Take a photocopy of the page and make mini flashcards. Place two chairs in front of the board, facing away from the board and towards the class. Position the other chairs in the class in two groups, each near the two chairs at the front.

**In class:** Divide your class into two teams. Each team has a chair and the rest of the team should sit near to that chair. One member from each team sits on the chairs at the front.

You then take one of the mini flashcards and stick it on the board. The two students on the chairs must not be able to see the picture on the card, but the rest of the teams can. The teams must then describe what the picture is. The first person on the chair to say the word correctly is the winner. Students must only use English, they should not mime and they cannot just point to the item!

***Example for beginner to elementary level:***
*You wear it on your head in the winter. It's made from wool. (card 3)*

***Example for more advanced levels:***
*You usually wear this with a suit. You put it round your neck and tie it in a knot. (card 8)*

## ③ Vocabulary builder: **Word halves**

**Level:** Beginner to pre-intermediate.

**Preparation:** Photocopy the pictures and make mini flashcards, enough for your students to work in groups of three. Cut out the cards, then cut the pictures in half. Now prepare word cards. Write the word halves (see below) on different pieces of paper and mix them up before you hand them out.

**In class:** Divide the class into groups. Give each group a set of pictures and the word halves. The first group to match the pictures and the word halves wins.

| *Word halves:* | |
|---|---|
| baseball | cap |
| beanie | hat |
| jump | er |
| scar | f |
| train | ers |
| sh | irt |
| T- | shirt |
| bla | zer |
| sports | bag |
| ruck | sack |
| trou | sers |
| t | ie |

## ④ Vocabulary: **Memory game**

**Level:**     Beginner to elementary.

**In class:**    Tell your students you are a famous football star. Drill this line with your class, and add an item of clothing to it: *I'm (Lionel Messi). I'm going to the World Cup and I'm taking my (sports bag).*

Go around the class and ask each student to add a new item of clothing to the last one.

*Example:*
*I'm (Lionel Messi). I'm going to the World Cup and I'm taking my sports bag and my scarf.*

How many items can they take before they forget something?

## ⑤ Speaking: **Shopping role-play**

**Level:**     This task can be adapted to any level.

**Preparation:**  Photocopy the pictures to make three sets of mini flashcards and cut out the cards. On two sets, write the same size (for example, *medium*) or a colour next to each item. On the other set, write a different size or colour.

**In class:**    Divide your students into shop assistants and customers. Give the shop assistants two sets of cards (with different sizes / colours on). Give the customers one or two flashcards each (depending on how many students you have). They must ask for the item on their flashcard by 'visiting' each shop assistant. If the shop assistant has the exact details they ask for (the item with the correct size / colour), they must give the card to the customer.

*Example for lower levels:*
**Customer:**     Have you got any T-shirts? I'm small.
**Sales assistant:** Yes, we have. Here you are. / No, sorry.

*Example for more advanced levels:*
**Customer:**     I'm looking for a red T-shirt. I'm a size 10.
**Sales assistant:** Sorry, we're out of stock. We've only got large T-shirts. Try another branch.

# Internet: Extra Time ▶

**Go to www.collinselt.com/football**

# Unit 17  The Fans

PHOTOCOPIABLE  English Through Football 978-0-00-752234-7  www.collinselt.com/football

# Target Language

## Describing people

### Hair
**Colour:** He's / She's got fair / blond / brown / ginger / dark / grey hair.
**Length:** He's / She's got short / mid-length / long hair. He's bald / a skinhead.
**Type:** He's / She's got straight / curly / wavy / spiky hair.
**Hair style:** He's / She's got a pony tail / a bun / plaits.

### Appearance
**Eyes:** He's / She's got blue / green / brown / grey eyes.
**Skin:** He's / She's got wrinkles / freckles / scars.
He's / She's got pale / fair / dark / tanned skin.
**Facial hair:** He's got stubble / a moustache / a beard / a goatee beard.
**Build:** He's / She's average build / slim / stocky / big.

### Age
He's / She's …
a baby / a toddler / a boy / a girl / a teenager / an adult.
in his / her teens / twenties / thirties / forties.
middle-aged / old / elderly / an OAP (= old-age pensioner).

### Clothes
He's / She's wearing …
a leather / denim jacket / a coat / an anorak / a shirt / a dress.
jeans / trousers / shorts / tracksuit bottoms.
a scarf / gloves / glasses / sunglasses / earrings.
a baseball cap / a bobble hat / a beanie hat / a novelty football hat.
shoes / boots / trainers.

### Clothes style
He's / She's … smart / sporty / casual / fashionable / stylish.

### Attitude
He / She looks …
happy / cheerful / friendly / funny / shy / serious / miserable / moody.

# Using the pictures

## 1 Reading: Match it!

**Level:** Elementary to intermediate.
**Preparation:** Photocopy the descriptions on page 70 or copy them on the board.
**In class:** Give your students the descriptions on the following page. You can adjust them according to your students' level. They match the descriptions to the correct flashcards. Note these descriptions are in the order of the cards so you may want to shuffle them.

This fan's a man in his twenties. He's got fair hair. He's wearing a striped shirt, jeans and a jacket. He's got a painted face. He looks cheerful.

This fan's a girl. She's wearing a a stripy football shirt, shorts, football socks and trainers. She's in her late teens or early twenties. She looks friendly.

This fan's in his sixties. He's wearing a scarf, hat and a thick coat. He's wearing glasses and he's got a moustache.

This fan's a young boy. He looks happy. He's wearing a beanie hat.

This fan's in his twenties. He's wearing a striped T-shirt, tight jeans and big boots. He's a skinhead.

This fan's in his forties. He's wearing a baseball cap. He's eating a pie and carrying a flag. He looks friendly and cheerful.

This fan's a girl. She's in her twenties or thirties. She's wearing big earrings.

This fan's in her sixties. She's got curly hair and is wearing glasses and a bobble hat. She's wearing a skirt, thick coat and boots.

This fan's a teenager. He's slim. He's wearing a scarf, a beanie hat and trainers. He looks shy.

**Extension:** You can add in a 'red herring' (a distractor). See if your students can find it!

This fan's in his twenties. He's wearing a striped shirt and trainers. He's wearing a novelty hat, sunglasses and is carrying a flag.

## ❷ Speaking and listening: Bingo

**Level:** Elementary to intermediate.

**Preparation:** Photocopy two sets of the mini flashcards – one at A4 size and the other enlarged to A3 size. Make sure the flashcard numbers are visible. Stick the enlarged A3 flashcards on the board. Cut up the A4 photocopied sheet so you have a set of flashcards and fold up each picture. Put these into a hat or a bag.

**In class:** Ask students to give each of the fans on the board an English name. Write the names under the pictures on the board. Now, ask each student to choose three fan flashcards and write down the names on a piece of paper.
One student should pull out a flashcard from the hat or bag. They must not show the card or say the name, but should describe the character to the class. If the description matches the name of the fan a student has chosen, they can tick it off. The game continues until one student has ticked off all three fans.

PHOTOCOPIABLE   English Through Football 978-0-00-752234-7   www.collinselt.com/football

## ③ Speaking and grammar: Who am I?

**Level:** Elementary.

**Preparation:** Photocopy the cards enough times so that you can stick one set of the mini flashcards on the board, and each of your students can also have a flashcard of one of the characters. You will also need some tape or pins to stick the cards on students' backs.

**In class:** Stick one of the characters on each student's back, so they cannot see who they are. Students should walk around the class, asking other students questions to find out who they are (but they must not ask directly for a card number). They can only ask one question to each class member. They can refer to the cards on the board to help them.

*Example:*

**Student A:** *Have I got a beard?*

**Student A:** *Am I female?*

**Student A:** *Am I wearing glasses?*

**Student A:** *Am I wearing shorts?*

**Student A:** *I know! I'm card 2!*

**Student B:** *No, you haven't.*

**Student C:** *Yes, you are.*

**Student D:** *No, you're not.*

**Student E:** *Yes, you are.*

**Variation:** Stick famous people's names or class members' names to each of your students.

## ④ Writing: A wanted poster

**Level:** Elementary to intermediate.

**Preparation:** Photocopy the 'Wanted' poster below.

**In class:** Ask your students to draw a person who is wanted by the police. They should write a description of the person using the target language and this poster.

# WANTED!

Name: _____ Age:_____

Description: _____

Wanted for: _____

If you see this person, call the police on: **9843000 675436426**

## Internet: Extra Time ▶

Go to **www.collinselt.com/football**

# Target Language

## Verbs

1. to read
2. to eat
3. to drink
4. to clap
5. to shout
6. to whistle
7. to sing
8. to cry
9. to hug
10. to celebrate / to cheer
11. to wave something
12. to play the drums

## Extra vocabulary

- to applaud
- to yell / jeer
- to chant
- to despair
- to embrace
- to jump for joy

# Using the pictures

## 1 Grammar: Pelmanism

**Level:** Beginner to intermediate.

**Preparation:** Photocopy and cut out the pictures to make 12 mini flaschards. Back these up with card to make sure students cannot cheat and see the picture through the paper. Then, make 12 blank cards and write out the 12 verbs in the present continuous (or infinitive form, if you prefer): *She's reading. He's eating. He's drinking. They're clapping. He's shouting.* etc.

**In class:** Jumble and place the word and picture cards face down in two piles. Ask a student to turn over a picture card, say the action in English and then turn over a word card. If the two cards match, the student keeps the cards and can pick two more cards. Otherwise, another student turns over two cards. The winner is the student with the most pairs.

## 2 Listening: Fans in the stand

**Level:** Beginnner to intermediate.

**In class:** Ask your students to stand in rows, as if watching a football match. Call out the situations below and get students to mime the actions they would do as real fans. Ask students to say what they are doing, using the present continuous.

*Examples for lower levels:*

**Teacher:** *You're hungry.*
**Students:** [*mime eating a burger*] *We're eating.*
**Teacher:** *You're thirsty.*
**Students:** [*mime having a drink*] *We're drinking.*
**Teacher:** *Your team are losing 5-0!*
**Students:** [*mime crying / leaving*] *We're crying. / We're going home!*
**Teacher:** *The game is slow and boring.*
**Students:** [*mime whistling / reading / playing drums*] *We're whistling. / We're reading the programme. / We're playing the drums.*

*Examples for intermediate levels:*
**Teacher:**     *Your team has just scored a goal!*
**Students:**    [*mime celebrating*] *We're jumping for joy. / We're clapping. / We're hugging each other.*
**Teacher:**     *Your team is playing very badly.*
**Students:**    [*mime being angry*] *We're shouting / whistling at the players.*

**Extension:**     Now go to Unit 41. Students describe the scene using the present continuous and then draw the faces of the fans in the terraces. They can describe how they feel.

*Examples:*
*This fan's bored. He's reading a book.*
*This fan's happy. She's cheering and shouting.*

## ❸ Writing: **Where else?**

**Level:**        Beginner to intermediate.
**In class:**     Show your students the mini flashcards one at a time. Ask them to write down as many other situations when or places where they would do these activities apart from at a football match. Give them a time limit of 30 seconds for each card. You can ask them the following questions (with suggested answers in brackets):

*When or where do you ...*
1. *read?* (in a school / library, on a bus / train, in bed etc.)
2. *drink?* (in a café / restaurant, at the gym, in the cinema etc.)
3. *clap?* (at an award ceremony, after a play / show / concert)
4. *shout?* (when you are angry, when you are in a noisy place such as a station or concert etc.)
5. *sing?* (in the shower / bath, at a concert, in a school assembly, in church, when you listen to the radio / your MP3 player etc.)
6. *cry?* (when you are sad / upset, in a sad movie, at a funeral etc.)
7. *hug somebody?* (when you say hello / goodbye, when you are scared, when you are in love etc.)
8. *celebrate?* (when you hear good news / pass an exam / win something etc.)

## ❹ Speaking: **Past simple game**

**Level:**        Beginner to intermediate.
**In class:**     Use this game to practise the past simple and past simple time indicators. First, elicit past simple time indicators using a calendar if necessary, e.g. *yesterday, last week, last year, two weeks ago, a month ago.* Check the meaning by asking concept questions: *What year was last year? What day was yesterday?*
Now, on the board write: *When did you last ...?*
Pick up one of the mini flashcards and get students to complete the sentence.

*Example:*
**Teacher:** [*shows card 8*]
**Students:** *When did you last cry?*

Now get them to answer the question using a past simple time indicator. If they answer, *two days ago,* ask more questions: *Why? Where were you?* etc.

**Extension:**     Divide your class into pairs. Give each pair a set of the mini flashcards. The students take it in turns to turn over a card and ask *When did you last ...?* , changing the verb according to the picture they have. Their partner answers.

## ⑤ Writing: Match report

**Level:**        Intermediate.
**Preparation:**  Photocopy or copy on the board the story below.
**In class:**     Students read the story and use the correct flashcards as prompts to complete the story.
**Variation:**    For lower levels, hold up the appropriate card for each gap to elicit correct answers. Suggested answers below.

---

### A Day at a London Football Game

Today I'm at Upton Park in East London. I'm watching West Ham. West Ham are playing Arsenal.

I arrive at the stadium and I feel hungry so I **[1]** _____. Then, I buy a programme and take my seat. I sit in the Bobby Moore Stand.

When the West Ham team comes out, everybody **[2]** _____ West Ham's song, *I'm Forever Blowing Bubbles*.

When the game starts, we **[3]** _____ and **[4]** _____.

But then Arsenal score. The fans are angry with the goalkeeper and they _____ **[5]** at him.

Two minutes later, there's another goal for Arsenal. "I want to **[6]** _____," says one of the fans.

At half-time, I go to the snack bar and I **[7]** _____, then I **[8]** _____ my programme.

The second half is different. West Ham score a goal and we **[9]** _____ , and then, just ten minutes later, there's another goal for West Ham. We **[10]** _____ each other.

Arsenal start to attack, but it's too late – the referee **[11]** _____. West Ham 2 Arsenal 2.

It's a draw!

---

**Suggested answers: 1.** card 2, eat a hamburger  **2.** card 7, sings / chants  **3.** card 4, clap  **4.** card 5, shout  **5.** card 5, shout  **6.** card 8, cry  **7.** card 3, have a drink  **8.** card 1, read  **9.** card 10, cheer  **10.** card 9, hug  **11.** card 6, whistles

**Extension:**    Students can use this model to write their own story about a match, using the picture cards as prompts.

## Internet: Extra Time ▶

### Go to www.collinselt.com/football

# Unit 19 People at the Ground

# Target Language

## Important people

1. a reporter
2. the captain
3. a player
4. the goalkeeper (goalie)
5. the referee (ref)
6. an assistant referee (linesman)
7. a substitute (sub)
8. the physiotherapist (physio)
9. the coach
10. the manager
11. the commentator
12. the photographer

## Extra vocabulary

- a sports reporter
- a police officer
- a steward (= a person who helps people at the stadium)
- a ticket tout (= a person who buys / sells football tickets illegally)
- the groundsman (= a person who looks after the pitch / grass)

# Using the pictures

## 1 Reading: Who says it?

**Level:** Elementary to intermediate.
**Preparation:** Photocopy or copy on the board the six phrases below.
**In class:** Students read the six phrases and match them with the appropriate mini flashcard.

> 1. You're booked! Next time, you'll get a red card!
> 2. No, it wasn't over the line. Play on!
> 3. Right, Jones. I want you to go in attack.
> 4. Oh no, you've broken your leg!
> 5. Can I take your picture, please?
> 6. Don't worry! I'll save this penalty.

## 2  Speaking: **What do you say?**

**Level:**          Elementary to intermediate.

**Preparation:**   Photocopy and cut out the mini flashcards enough times so your students can work in pairs. Shuffle the cards and divide them into two.

**In class:**       Place students in pairs. Student A takes one half of the cards, Student B takes the other. At the same time, both students turn over the top card. They look at the people on the cards and decide what they would say to each other. Monitor and write up any good examples of English you hear on the board.
*Example:*
**Student A:** [*turns over card 12*] Can I take your photo?
**Student B:** [*turns over card 10*] No, I'm busy talking to my team.

**Extension:**      Ask students to continue one of their dialogues and act it out.


## 3  Listening: **It's in the bag!**

**Level:**          Elementary to intermediate.

**In class:**       Put the mini flashcards on the board. Ask students what these people take to work. Tell them they will now hear some of the people's descriptions of what they have in their work bags. Students match what they hear to the correct card. Read the following descriptions (suggested answers in brackets):

1. *In my bag, I've got my kit – it's black and white. I've also got my whistle. I've got a notebook and two cards: a red card and yellow card.* (card 5)
2. *In my bag, I've got a sponge, some ice, a bandage and some tablets.* (card 8)
3. *In my bag, I've got my football kit and my gloves.* (card 4)
4. *In my bag, I've got my kit – it's black and white. I've also got a flag.* (card 6)
5. *In my bag, I've got my camera.* (card 12)
6. *In my bag, I've got my notebook and pencil, a DVD of the other team and I've got my suit and tie.* (card 10)
7. *In my bag, I've got a notebook, my microphone and my glasses.* (card 1 or 11)

**Extension:**      Students write the content of their own bag on a piece of paper and give the paper to you. Redistribute the pieces of paper to the rest of the class. Students read out what is on their paper and the rest of the class must guess whose bag it is.

**Variation:**      For more advanced levels, give students these other professions. Ask students to suggest what they carry in their bags: a teacher, a detective, a paramedic / doctor, a model, a hairdresser.


## 4  Writing: **A day in their life ...**

**Level:**          Elementary to intermediate.

**In class:**       Ask students to choose one of the people from the mini flashcards. Now they write about their day. They can use the following framework which you can copy on the board.

*A day in my life*
- *I'm a ...*
- *I arrive at the match at ...*
- *I wear ...*
- *I need to bring ...*
- *My role is to ...*
- *The best part of my job is ...*

**Variation:**   To practise past tenses, students can write about a particular day using the past simple or past continuous.

*Example:*
*I'm a goalie. Yesterday, I arrived at nine o'clock. The first thing I did at the stadium was to put on my gloves.*

## ⑤ Speaking and writing: My football stadium

**Level:**   This activity works best with younger learners of any level.

**In class:**   Ask students to create their own football stadium using the mini flashcards. Refer them to the pitch outline in Unit 42. Now ask them to position their flashcards on or around the pitch in any way they like so it represents a real football stadium.
When they have finished, they can describe their stadium to their partner.

*Example:*
*In my stadium, the reporter is standing next to the goalie. A player is taking a penalty. The manager is looking happy.*

**Extension:**   Students can write a description of their stadium for homework.

## Internet: Extra Time ▶

Go to www.collinselt.com/football

# Target Language

## Verbs

1. to stand
2. to shake hands
3. to run
4. to jump
5. to throw
6. to kick / pass
7. to dive
8. to tackle
9. to push
10. to foul
11. to lie (on the ground)
12. to argue (with the ref)

## Extra vocabulary

- to volley
- to save
- to shove
- to trip someone up

# Using the pictures

## 1 Listening: Hold up!

**Level:** Elementary to intermediate.

**Preparation:** Photocopy and cut out the mini flashcards enough times for your students to work in pairs or alone.

**In class:** Ask students to spread out the mini flashcards on the table in front of them. Now read out the situations below. Students listen and hold up the appropriate card (suggested answers in brackets):

1. *What do you do before the match?* (card 2)
2. *What do you do when you are angry about the referee's decision?* (card 12)
3. *What do you do to stop a player with the ball?* (card 8)
4. *What do you do when you hurt your leg?* (card 11)
5. *What do you do after the ball goes off the pitch?* (card 5)
6. *What do you do when you try to stop the ball going in the net?* (card 7)

**Variation:** If you have younger students, photocopy and enlarge one set of cards only. Stick the cards around the classroom. Students should listen to your descriptions and stand by that card. For lower levels, you could just shout out the action, e.g. *kick*. Students run to that card.

**Extension:** To follow up, ask students to choose a verb from the mini flashcards. They mime doing the verb to a partner, but using a non-football situation. The other students then guess the verb.

## ② Speaking: **Where else?**

**Level:** Elementary to intermediate.

**In class:** Show your students the mini flashcards one at a time. Ask them to say as many other situations when or places where they would do these activities apart from at a football match. You can ask them the following questions (with suggested answers in brackets):

***When or where do you ...***

1. *shake hands with someone?* (when you meet someone for the first time; after an award show; with your boss in the office; at an interview; when you agree a price or a deal; before or after a game or sport)
2. *run?* (when you are late; when you are playing a game; when you want to keep fit)
3. *throw something?* (when you want someone to catch something; at a sports event you throw a javelin / discus; when you have litter you throw it in the bin)
4. *kick something?* (when you are angry; you kick leaves in autumn; you may kick yourself when you make a silly mistake)
5. *dive?* (at a swimming pool; in the sea)
6. *push something?* (some people push in queues and to get on buses and trains; you can push a child in a pushchair; you push a child in a swing; you can push a car or a bike; you push a door open)
7. *lie on the ground?* (when you are tired or ill; on a beach or in a park)
8. *argue with someone?* (when you don't agree with them; when you are angry)

**Extension:** Give students the following gapped sentences. They can complete them with the correct verbs. (Suggested answers in brackets.)

1. *I'm tired. I'm going to _____ on my bed.* (lie)
2. *It's hot. I want to go to the pool and _____ in the water.* (dive)
3. *My friend has got a trampoline. The kids love to _____ on it.* (jump)
4. *I'm late. I must _____ to the bus stop.* (run)
5. *Hey, wait until everybody gets off the train. Don't _____.* (push)
6. *Be careful standing next to those horses. They can _____.* (kick)

## ③ Conjunctions: **What happens next?**

**Level:** Intermediate.

**Preparation:** Copy or write the sentence halves opposite on card and stick them to the left- and right-hand side of the board. Write the conjunctions below on different coloured pieces of card.

**In class:** Show students the following conjunctions (you can choose / explain these depending on their level).

> **Conjunctions**
>
> **Result:** *and, so*
> **Time:** *then, next, a minute later, seconds later, after that*
> **Contrast:** *but, yet, however, although, in spite of this*

Ask students to match the sentences and to complete them with a suitable correct conjunction. Feedback and check the answers.

| | |
|---|---|
| 1. The players shake hands | a ... the striker gets a free kick. |
| 2. The goalkeeper dives for the ball | b ... the doctor comes on the pitch. |
| 3. The defender fouls the striker | c ... the game kicks off. |
| 4. The captain argues with the referee | d ... he saves it. |
| 5. A player lies on the ground | e ... the referee does not book the captain. |

*Suggested answers:*

1. The players shake hands. **After that / Then** the game kicks off.
2. The goalkeeper dives for the ball **and** he saves it.
3. The defender fouls the striker, **so** the striker gets a free kick.
4. The captain argues with the referee, **but** the referee does not book the captain. / **In spite of this**, the referee does not book the captain.
5. A player lies on the ground. **A minute later,** the doctor comes on the pitch.

**Extension:** Put your students into pairs and give each a set of mini flashcards. They can choose up to five cards to make a mini story. They should try and use the conjunctions to link their sentences.

## Internet: Extra Time ▶

Go to **www.collinselt.com/football**

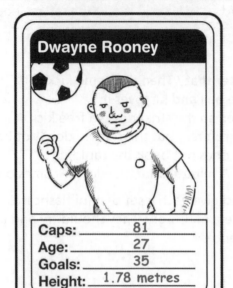

**Dwayne Rooney**

Caps: 81
Age: 27
Goals: 35
Height: 1.78 metres

**Peckham Beckham**

Caps: 115
Age: 37
Goals: 17
Height: 1.82 metres

**Bernando Torres**

Caps: 101
Age: 29
Goals: 31
Height: 1.76 metres

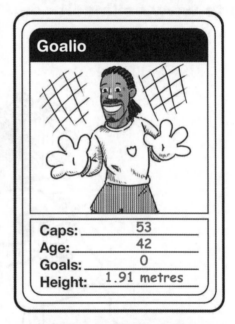

**Goalio**

Caps: 53
Age: 42
Goals: 0
Height: 1.91 metres

**Gareth Dale**

Caps: 74
Age: 29
Goals: 34
Height: 1.86 metres

**Van Mersie**

Caps: 53
Age: 23
Goals: 57
Height: 1.86 metres

# Target Language

## Describing the players

1. He's fast / quick / speedy.
2. He's tall and strong / small and powerful.
3. He's very athletic / imposing / tough.
4. He has good stamina / is very fit.
5. He's intelligent / sharp / alert / quick-thinking.
6. He's playing well / on (good) form.
7. He's really talented / skilful / creative / adept.

## Football phrases: Technical terms

- He's right- / left-footed.
- He can use both feet.
- He's good at headers / corners / free kicks / set pieces / tackles.

## Team work

- a team-player
- a captain / a leader
- a hard worker
- selfish

## Experience

- He / She has made one hundred appearances for his / her club.
- He / She has two international caps. (= international appearances)

# Using the pictures

## 1 Speaking: Trumps

**Level:** This game can be adapted to any level.

**In class:** Divide the class into pairs. Each student takes three mini flashcards each. They look at their cards, but must not show them to their partner.

Student A puts down a card and names one of the categories (caps, age, goals or height) and reads what his card says.

*Example:*
*Van Mersie has got 74 caps.*

Student B looks at his / her card to see if it can 'trump' or beat this number of caps (or whatever category Student A chose). So if Student B has 'Peckham Beckham' with 115 caps, this card wins.

Player B then takes the next card and calls another category on their card. The winner of the game is the player with the most cards.

| **Variation:** | For more advanced students, players can compare their cards using the comparative form. |
| --- | --- |
| | ***Examples:*** |
| | *Bernando Torres has got more goals than Goalio. Goalio is taller than Dwayne Rooney. Van Mersie is older than Gareth Dale.* |
| **Extension:** | After students are familiar with the game, students can draw or find photos of players (in magazines, online, in newspapers etc.) and stick them on the blank cards (see Unit 43) to make additional cards. Students can write the categories for their player. |
| **Variation:** | More advanced students can write different categories, e.g. Fitness, Skill Level, Popularity, Looks, Leadership etc. Students can compare the players. |
| | ***Example:*** |
| | *Klose is much quicker than Ballack. Cole is fitter than Podolski and is a better team player etc.* |
| | A further variation is to compare six teams (number of trophies, age, etc.), or six stadia (capacity, value, date they were built etc.). |

## ❷ Listening: Hold up!

| **Level:** | Elementary to intermediate. |
| --- | --- |
| **Preparation:** | Photocopy the pictures and make enough sets of mini flashcards for your students to work in pairs or small groups. |
| **In class:** | Students lay out the cards in front of them. Then ask students the following questions to practise the superlative. The students should find and hold up the correct card as quickly as possible (suggested answers in brackets): |
| | 1. *Which player is the oldest?* (Goalio) |
| | 2. *Which player is the most experienced?* (Peckham Beckham) |
| | 3. *Which player is the youngest?* (Bernando Torres) |
| | 4. *Which player has scored the most goals?* (Bernando Torres) |
| | 5. *Which player has scored the least goals?* (Goalio) |
| **Variation:** | You can also ask open-ended questions where students can choose a player and explain their choice: |
| | 1. *Which player do you think is the best-looking?* |
| | 2. *Which player do you think is the fastest? Why?* |
| | 3. *Which player do you think is the toughest? Why?* |
| | 4. *Which player do you think is the richest? Why?* |
| **Extension:** | Ask your students to order themselves into a line, according to these categories: |
| | *Who is the tallest in the class?* |
| | *Who is the oldest / youngest in the class?* |
| | *Who is the fastest in the class?* |
| | *Who lives the furthest away from / closest to school?* |
| | *Who is the loudest / quietest in the class?* |

## ❸ Speaking: How much?

| **Level:** | Elementary to intermediate. |
| --- | --- |
| **In class:** | Football players are very expensive to buy! Tell your students they are football managers and that the players on the mini flashcards are in their team. They must value these players before they sell or 'transfer' them. But how much are they worth? Give students these six amounts of money. |

> £200 million
> £100 million
> £80 million
> £50 million
> £20 million
> £10 million

Which players do they think is worth the most? Which player is worth the least? Students should rank their players using the comparative or the superlative forms.

**Example:**
**Student A:** *I think ... is worth £200 million. He has the most caps!*
**Student B:** *No, I think ... is worth £200 million. He has scored more goals and is younger than ...*

Students write their final fee on the back of the cards. Feedback as a class. Do they agree on the prices?

## ④ Role play: Boasting

**Level:**       Elementary to intermediate.
**In class:**    Give each student a mini flashcard. The student now becomes that player and will meet other players. Students should imagine it is the first time these players have met. They should mingle around the class asking each other questions, answering and 'showing off' as much as possible. Elicit questions, answers and reactions. For lower levels, you can give them these prompts:

| | |
|---|---|
| *How old are you?* | *I'm ...* |
| *How tall are you?* | *About ...* |
| *How many goals have you scored?* | *I've scored ...* |
| *Is that all? I've scored ...* | |
| *Have you got any caps?* | *I've got ...* |
| *Well, I've got ...* | |

## ⑤ Speaking: Top trumps

**Level:**        This can be adapted for any level.
**Preparation:** Photocopy the blank cards from Unit 43 enough times so you can give each student a card.
**In class:**    Students draw themselves on the cards or attach a photo of themselves. Then discuss and decide categories that you and your class think makes a top student.

**Examples:**
*A top student always arrives on time.*
*A top student always does his / her homework.*
*A top student always puts his / her hand up to answer.*

Ask students to write these categories on the cards:

> **On time:**
> **Homework in:**
> **In class behaviour:**

Collect in the cards. Tell students that at the end of each week, you'll give them a Top Trump score out of ten. Mark these on the cards in pencil. On the final lesson of the week, place the cards on the wall. Students can then see who was the Top Trump that week. The Top Trump students should be rewarded with a privilege or prize.

# Unit 22 Prepositions: Spot the Ball

PHOTOCOPIABLE   English Through Football 978-0-00-752234-7   www.collinselt.com/football

# Target Language

## Describing position

1. **in** the drawer
2. **on** his head
3. **behind** the computer
4. **over** the fence
5. **on** the shelf
6. **in** the cupboard
7. **under** the table
8. **in front of** the bin
9. **in between** the tables
10. **behind** the door
11. **next to** the cat
12. **on** his foot

# Using the pictures

## 1 Grammar: Do it!

**Level:** Beginner to intermediate.

**In class:** Go through each preposition, then give students instructions to check their understanding.

*Example:*

**Teacher:** *Put your pen on the table. Put your pencil on your head. Put your pen under the chair. Put your pen in your bag. Put your pen behind your back! etc.*

**Extension:** Now ask students to give each other instructions using prepositions and other classroom items.

## 2 Vocabulary: Snap!

**Level:** Beginner to intermediate.

**Preparation:** Photocopy and write the prepositions on the blank card templates (Unit 43). Photocopy the pictures and make mini flashcards, enough times for your students to work in pairs. Each pair now has a set of the mini flashcards and the preposition word cards.

**In class:** Divide students into pairs. They put the two sets of cards next to each other, face down. They then turn over the cards and place them down at the same time. If the picture and the word card matches, they must shout *Snap!* The first person to say *Snap!* keeps the cards. Continue until there are no cards left, or set a time limit. The person with the most cards is the winner.

### ③ Speaking: **Under the bed**

**Level:** Intermediate.

**Preparation:** Write a list of famous people that your students will know (actors, pop stars, football players, politicians etc.). Photocopy the list or copy it on the board.

**In class:** Ask students these questions:

**Teacher:** *What can you find…*
*in your drawer?*
*in your bin?*
*on your shelf?*
*in your cupboard?*
*under your bed?*
*in your wardrobe?*

Now put students into pairs. Give Student A the name of a famous person. They should think about the kind of things that this person owns. Student B is going to guess the name of this person. They must think of questions about things that the famous person has in his / her house using the prepositions / furniture above. Now students work in pairs.

*Example:*
**Student B:** *What's in this person's cupboard?*
**Student A:** *A broom.*
**Student B:** *What's in this person's drawer?*
**Student A:** *A pair of glasses.*
**Student B:** *What's under this person's bed?*
**Student A:** *A book of spells.*
**Student B:** *Is it Harry Potter?*
**Student A:** *Yes, it is!*

### ④ Speaking and reading: **Find the footballs**

**Level:** This activity works best with lower level young learners.

**Preparation:** Photocopy and cut out the football below 12 times. Before the lesson, 'hide' the balls around your classroom. The balls should be positioned to practise the prepositions (i.e. *under the table, on the board, in the bin, under the window*). You can adapt the table on the following page according to your classroom. Then photocopy it enough times for each of your students to have a copy.

**In class:** Give each of your students a table. Tell your students they have to find the footballs. They should tick where they are in the class. At the end, they tell you where they found the footballs, using the information in the table on the following page.

| The Football is … | on | in | under | behind | in front of | next to |
|---|---|---|---|---|---|---|
| the table | | | | | | |
| the chair | | | | | | |
| the bin | | | | | | |
| the window | | | | | | |
| the blackboard | | | | | | |
| the door | | | | | | |

## ⑤ Speaking: Spot the ball

**Level:** Beginner to intermediate.

**Preparation:** Find a photo of a football scene from a newspaper or a magazine without a ball in it. Now add grid lines and axis (1-10 vertically and A-J horizontally). Photocopy this picture enough times so each student has the same picture.

**In class:** Divide your students into pairs. Give each student a picture. Each pair should put up a 'screen' between them (for example a book or a ringbinder). On one picture, each player marks where their football is. Then each student must try and find the other player's football. They take it in turns to ask questions. Demonstrate the questions to your class before they play. Students must try to use a preposition in their questions.

*Example:*
**Student A:** *Is your football on player number ten's head?*
**Student B:** *No, it isn't.*
**Student A:** *Is your football in the goal?*
**Student B:** *No, it isn't.*
**Student A:** *Is your football in square G1?*
**Student B:** *Yes, it is!*

 **Internet: Extra Time ▶**

**Go to www.collinselt.com/football**

# Target Language

## Describing the players: prepositions of place

1. next to
2. behind
3. in front of
4. between
5. in the front row
6. in the back row
7. in the middle row
8. in the middle
9. at the end
10. on the left / right
11. the second / third person on the right
12. the second / third person on the left

# Using the pictures

## 1 Listening: Who is it?

**Level:** Beginner to intermediate.

**Preparation:** Photocopy the picture enough times for you and each of your students. On your copy, write names next to each of the players.

**In class:** Give out a picture to each of your students. Then read out descriptions, giving your students the position each player is sitting in. Students identify each person.

*Example:*
*Seb Striker is standing at the end in the back row. He's got blond hair. Can you see him?*

## 2 Speaking and listening: Information gap

**Level:** Beginner to intermediate.

**Preparation:** Before the lesson, photocopy the picture and write names next to all of the football players in the picture. Put this to one side. Now photocopy a clean version of the picture twice, and label each A and B. On picture A, write half of your names. Write the rest of your names on picture B. Photocopy pictures A and B enough times so half of your students can be A and half can be B.

**In class:** Divide your class into A and B. Give Student A picture A and Student B picture B. They must not show each other their pictures. Tell students they should find out all of the names of the team on the picture by asking their partner questions using prepositions of place.

*Example:*
**Student A:** *Who is sitting in the front row, in the middle?*
**Student B:** *It's Paolo. OK. Who is next to Paolo, on his left?*

They can check their answers with each other's pictures or by looking at the completed version you prepared.

### 3 Speaking: Talk about the team

**Level:** Beginner to intermediate.
**Preparation:** Ask students to bring in a photo showing their favourite team (or the cast of a TV show or film they like).
**In class:** Students use their photo to talk to their partner, using the prepositions of place.

*Example:*
**Student A:** *This is Andrea Pirlo, he's in the middle. He's got brown hair. Next to him is Mario Balotelli.*
**Student B:** *Who is that behind Mario Balotelli?*
**Student A:** *That's Gianluigi Buffon!*

### 4 Speaking: My old school photo

**Level:** Beginner to intermediate.
**Preparation:** Bring in an old school photo of yourself in class (if you have one!). Also, before the lesson, ask students to bring in a school class photo of themselves when they were younger.
**In class:** Ask students to find you in the photo. They should not just point, but ask questions to work out where you are sitting using the prepositions of place.

*Example:*
**Student A:** *Are you in the back row?*
**Student B:** *Are you next to the girl with blonde hair?*

If they cannot guess, describe where you are.

*Example:*
**Teacher:** *I'm in the front row. I'm sitting between the tall boy and the girl with ginger hair.*

**Extension:** Ask your students to guess who was …
1. your best friend?
2. the class bully?
3. your girlfriend / boyfriend?
4. the class genius?

*Example:*
*Was your best friend the girl sitting in the back row behind the teacher?*

Now students should present their old school photos to the rest of the class. The other students can ask questions.

*Examples:*
*Who is the boy next to you?*
*Who is sitting behind you?*
*Which one is / was your best friend?*

### 5 Speaking and listening: Spot the difference

**Level:** This can be adapted to any level.
**Preparation:** You will need to bring two large A3 pieces of paper to the lesson and make sure there is some space in the classroom for students to gather for a 'team photo'.
**In class:** Divide students into A and B. Team A takes a sheet of paper and faces the wall. They must not look at Team B. In the meantime, Team B should arrange themselves as if they were in a team photo, and hold the position. One member from Team A can now look at Team B. They should describe the group to the rest of their team.

*Example:*
*There are three rows of three people. In the back row, there is Janek on the left, Ania in the middle and Dariusz at the end.*

The rest of team A should listen. Together they draw a picture of how team B are standing. They have two minutes to complete the task, then they look to see if they have drawn Team B correctly. Now teams swap over and repeat the task.

**Variation:** Ask all students except one to arrange themselves into a team photo. The other student looks away.

Now the remaining student can look at the class team for ten seconds only. S/he must then stand outside the classroom. Then the class team photo must 'rearrange' itself – so at least two students should swap places. After 30 seconds, the student outside knocks to come in. S/he must guess what has changed.

*Example:*
*I know! Carla and Monica are in different places. Carla was next to Federico, but now she's next to Andrea. And Monica was in the first row, but now she's in the back row!*

## ⑥ Writing: **Our class photo**

**Level:** Elementary to advanced.
**Preparation:** Take a photo of your class. Upload it to your computer and print it for the class.
**In class:** Students should write a caption for the photo using the prepositions of place. They can also write fun facts about their classmates, too. They can use the following model:

*Example:*
*In the front row you can see Zoe, Mike and Sarah. At the end on the left it's Zoe. Zoe loves dogs. She's crazy about them! Mike is sitting in the middle – he's a brilliant bike rider. Sarah is sitting on the right. Did you know that she's a big football fan?*

## Internet: **Extra Time** ▶

**Go to www.collinselt.com/football**

**Prepositions: Photocall**   **95**

# Target Language

## Daily routine

1. I get up at eight o'clock.
2. I have a big breakfast.
3. I drive to the training ground.
4. I train for an hour.
5. We have a meeting with the manager. We discuss tactics.
6. I put on my kit.
7. I play football.
8. I do interviews.
9. I have a shower.
10. I put on my clothes and do my hair.
11. I go to a club.
12. I go to bed.

## Daily routine phrases

- I wake up at …
- I jump out of bed.
- I have a lie-in.

- I get dressed.
- I put on my make up / coat / clothes …

## Washing and grooming

- I have a wash.
- I have a bath / shower.
- I brush my teeth.

- I comb / brush / dry my hair
- I have a shave.

## Leaving for work and school

- I leave the house at …
- I walk / go on foot to …

- I take the train / tube / bus to …
- I drive to …

## Food

- I have lunch / tea / dinner at …
- I have a snack / break at …

## After work

- I watch TV / DVDs.
- I surf the Internet / go online / chat to my friends.

- I go to the gym.
- I do homework.
- I meet my friends.

# Using the pictures

## 1 Vocabulary: Mime it

**Level:** Beginner to intermediate.

**In class:** Present the target language using TPR (total physical response) – students say the words and do the action. Then put students into pairs. They take it in turns to pick a mini flashcard and mime what it shows to their partner, without saying the words. The partner guesses the verb.

## 2 Grammar: Sequencing

**Level:** Elementary to intermediate.

**In class:** Put students into pairs. They must put the cards in order to show a football player's match day. After three minutes, feedback and collect their ideas, asking students to suggest the most likely order.

**Extension:** Give students the twelve blank cards from Unit 43. They should personalise these, drawing pictures of their own daily routine. They should then swap their cards with their partner. Each partner should ask questions and make sentences about their partner's day.

*Example:*
**Student A:** *Do you get up at 8 o'clock?*
**Student B:** *Yes, I do.*

## 3 Speaking: My day

**Level:** Beginner to intermediate.

**In class:** Students use the mini flashcards (or their pictures from activity 2 above) to talk about their own day. You can write the following as a model:

*Example:*
*I get up at six o'clock.*
*I put on my school uniform.*
*I have a big / light breakfast. I eat toast and I drink tea / juice.*
*I drive / walk / ride my bike to …*
*I have lunch at …*
*I finish school / work at …*

**Variation:** Ask students: *How does your routine change at the weekend? Do you get up at the same time? Do you eat the same things? Do you go to bed early or late?*

**Extension:** Follow up by asking students to write up their daily routine using linking phrases and conjunctions: *then, next, after that, later* etc.

## 4 Speaking: Objects

**Level:** Beginner to intermediate.

**Preparation:** Before the lesson, ask students to bring in five objects / realia that represent part of their daily routines. Do the same for yourself.

**In class:** Show students your five objects. For example, show an alarm clock with the hands set at 7.30am, some shower gel, a train ticket, a school book, a DVD. Students should then look at the objects and make guesses about your typical daily routine.

*Example:*

*You get up at half past seven, then you have a shower. After that, you take the train to work.*

Now, students show their objects and the rest of the class / their partners make similar sentences.

**Variation:** Instead of objects, you could record sound effects to show your daily routine: an alarm clock, running water, a hairdryer, etc. Students guess the verbs. Alternatively, give your students daily routine sentences and ask students to do appropriate sound effects.

## ⑤ Writing: Day in the life of ...

**Level:** Elementary to advanced.
**In class:** Students can choose another person and write about their imaginary day using the target language as a guide. They could write about one of the following:
1. A famous Hollywood actor
2. A member of the Royal Family
3. A police officer
4. A homeless person
5. A pet dog or cat

## ⑥ Grammar: Around the world

**Level:** Beginner to intermediate.
**Preparation:** Bring in a clock and a map of the world with the time zones on it.
**In class:** Show your students the time zones and give them the time differences.

> For example, in London, England (Greenwich Mean Time = GMT) it's 9am.
> • In Berlin, Germany, it's + 1 hour. It's 10am.
> • In Athens, Greece, it's + 2 hours. It's 11am.
> • In Sydney, Australia, it's + 11 hours. It's 8pm.
> • In New York, U.S.A, it's − 5 hours, so it's 4am.

Now go around the class, asking students what they are doing. They make sentences using the present continuous.

*Example:*
**Teacher:** *It's eight o'clock in London. I'm having breakfast.*
*Paulo, you're in Greece. What time is it and what are you doing?*
**Student:** *It's ten o'clock. I'm in school!*

**Extension:** To follow up, ask students to choose a time. They then draw five clocks, one for each of the time zones above, and write what five people are doing at that point of time.

# Target Language

## Describing a day

1. I left home at 2pm.
2. I caught the bus.
3. I arrived at the stadium. I waited in the queue.
4. I bought / collected my ticket.
5. I bought a programme.
6. I drank a cola.
7. I found my seat and sat down.
8. Chelsea got a goal. One-nil!
9. I had / ate a burger at half-time.
10. I took my seat again.
11. The defender kicked the striker.
12. The referee gave Chelsea a penalty. Two-nil!
13. The referee gave the defender a red card / sent the defender off!
14. Chelsea got another goal. Three-nil!
15. The referee blew his whistle. Chelsea won 3-0!
16. The fans were delighted!

# Using the pictures

## 1 Grammar: Bash the board

**Level:** Beginner to intermediate.
**Preparation:** Before the class, write on the board or copy the table below. Find two magazines / newspapers. Roll and fix them into a stick shape.

| Present | Past tense? | |
|---|---|---|
| 1. **give** | ☐ gave | ☐ good |
| 2. **take** | ☐ took | ☐ tock |
| 3. **catch** | ☐ caught | ☐ cat |
| 4. **get** | ☐ gut | ☐ got |
| 5. **buy** | ☐ bought | ☐ but |
| 6. **leave** | ☐ left | ☐ leaf |
| 7. **blow** | ☐ blew | ☐ below |
| 8. **have** | ☐ had | ☐ hat |
| 9. **eat** | ☐ at | ☐ ate |
| 10. **are** | ☐ were | ☐ was |
| 11. **drink** | ☐ drank | ☐ drunk |
| 12. **find** | ☐ fan | ☐ found |
| 13. **send** | ☐ sent | ☐ sand |

**In class:** Divide your class into two teams. The teams should stand in two lines facing the board. Give the first team member of each team a 'stick'. Then call out one of the verbs in its present form. The students should run to the board and 'bash' or hit the correct past tense form with the stick. The player to hit the correct word first gets a goal for their team. If you hit the wrong word it is a 'miss' and a minus one goal.

## ② Grammar: Past tense pass

**Level:** Beginner to intermediate.
**Preparation:** Bring in a small, soft ball.
**In class:** Divide students into two teams. They can stand in a circle, in any order. You stand in the middle and call out a present tense infinitive from the list of verbs. As you do so, throw the ball to one of the students. As soon as they touch the ball, they must say the past simple form and throw it back to you. If a student gets the answer correct, they can stay standing. If they get it wrong, they must sit down. The winner is the last student left standing.

## ③ Grammar: Past tense pelmanism

**Level:** Beginner to intermediate.
**Preparation:** Write the correct past and present forms of the verbs on page 101 on the templates (see Unit 43). Photocopy enough times for students to work in groups.
**In class:** Place two sets of the same mini flashcards face down on the table. Students take it in turns to turn over two cards. They should say the name of the verbs on the card, for example *give* and *bought*. If they turn over two cards that match, such as *give* and *gave*, they can keep them and can choose again. Otherwise they put them back in the same position. As the game progresses, students try to remember where the cards are to get matching pairs.

## ④ Speaking: Sequencing

**Level:** Elementary to intermediate.
**Preparation:** Photocopy the mini flashcards enough times so there is one set for each pair of students in your class. Make sure you cross out or cover the numbers on the pictures before you photocopy.
**In class:** Students work in pairs and order the cards to make a story. Feedback and elicit the stories, feeding in any language as you go.
**Variation:** Lower level students can tell the story using the present simple.
**Extension:** To follow up, give each pair the target language sentences. They match the sentences to each frame.

## ⑤ Writing: Substitution

**Level:** Elementary to intermediate.
**Preparation:** Before the lesson, photocopy the pictures and choose some frames to 'white-out' using a whitening correction pen. Here are some suggestions:

- White-out the fan's face – students can draw a different fan or themselves.
- White-out the time in frame 1. Students can draw a different time on the clock.
- White-out the cans of cola and the hamburger. Students can draw in different food or drink that the fan buys.
- White-out the programme and ask students to draw something different that the fan buys.

- White-out the goal and goalkeeper in frame 12 and ask students to draw whether the goalkeeper saves the penalty or not!
- White-out the final three frames and ask students to draw a different ending.

Now photocopy the blanked pictures and make mini flashcards, enough so that you have enough cards for each student.

**In class:** Give your student the flashcards and ask each student to personalise their story. For homework, they can write up their new story.

# 6 Speaking: **Back home**

**Level:** Intermediate. This activity works best if your students are familiar with the story and the verbs. It revises past simple question forms.

**Preparation:** Photocopy the pictures enough times for half of your class to have a set of mini flashcards. Then write the question prompts below on the board.

**In class:** Divide your class into pairs. Give a set of the story flashcards to Student B who has just been to a match. Student A is the wife / girlfriend / mum who cannot see the cards. Student A wants to ask many questions about the match. Ask them to refer to the question prompts and to continue the conversation:

- *How was it?*
- *How did you get to the stadium?*
- *What did you buy there?*
- *Did you have anything to eat?*
- *Did you have anything to drink?*
- *Who did you sit next to?*
- *What was the score?*
- *Who scored?*
- *Was it a good match?*

*Example:*
**Student A:** *Hello, honey / Mum, I'm home!*
**Student B:** *Oh great. How was it?*

Student A answers. At first they can use the flashcards for each answer, but then they could answer freely using their own ideas.

# 7 Listening: **What's he saying?**

**Level:** Intermediate.
**In class:** Read out these phrases. Students write down the number of the card.

1. *What a great match! Three goals – a fantastic win!* (card 16)
2. *That's the whistle. Full time! It's three–nil to Chelsea!* (card 15)
3. *A single to Stamford Bridge, please.* (card 2)
4. *Good afternoon. Can I collect my ticket, please? My surname is Townsend.* (card 4)
5. *Wow! Look at this queue for tickets!* (card 3)
6. *We're playing well! I can't wait for the second half!* (card 10)
7. *This is my seat. Hello! I'm Andy. I'm looking forward to the game. Are you?* (card 7)
8. *Can I have a cola please?* (card 6)
9. *Yes! It's another goal! Three-nil! It's a hat-trick for Drogba!* (card 14)
10. *One programme, please.* (card 5)
11. *Drogba takes the penalty ... and scores! Two-nil!* (card 12)
12. *Yes! Goal! One-nil!* (card 8)
13. *Goodbye! I'm leaving now. See you later!* (card 1)
14. *And Ferdinand gets a red card!* (card 13)
15. *Yum! This hamburger's delicious!* (card 9)
16. *That's a foul! Penalty!* (card 11)

# Unit 26  Ouch! Injuries

# Target Language

## Injuries

1. He's hurt his head.
2. He's got a nosebleed.
3. He's twisted his ankle.
4. He's hurt his hand.
5. He's hurt his shoulder.
6. He's hurt his leg.
7. He's hurt his toe. / His toe's swollen.
8. He's broken his arm.
9. He's hurt his back. / He's got backache.
10. He's hurt his finger. / His finger's swollen.
11. He's hurt his knee.
12. He's broken his leg.

## Extra vocabulary

### Verbs

- have got (an injury, a disease or a pain): *I've got a headache / stomachache / toothache.*
- to break (a bone): *He's broken his finger.*
- to injure / damage / hurt (a body part): *I've injured / damaged / hurt my shoulder.*
- to twist (an ankle / knee): *I've twisted my ankle.*
- to pull (a muscle): *I've pulled a muscle.*
- to strain (a muscle or body part): *I've strained my back.*
- to dislocate (a joint): *I've dislocated my shoulder / knee.*

## People

- a doctor
- a paramedic
- a first-aider
- a physio (physiotherapist)
- a patient

## Doctor's questions

- What's the matter?
- What happened?
- Where does it hurt?
- Can you move your leg / neck / hand / finger?
- It looks like / it might be (a broken / twisted) …

# Using the pictures

## 1 Vocabulary: Body parts

**Level:** Beginner to intermediate.
**Preparation:** Before you present the language for injuries, you will need to recycle the vocabulary for body parts. Here are two warmer games. Both of these games work best in younger, established classes where your students are familiar with each other.

**In class:** Divide your class into pairs and ask them to stand in a space, with their backs touching. This is 'back to back'. Now call out another body part, e.g. *hand to hand*. Students must touch hands as quickly as possible and hold the pose. Continue with more body parts, going faster and faster, e.g. *foot to foot, arm to arm, shoulder to shoulder* etc.

**Variation:** You will need a large pack of 'post-it' notes for this game. On the post-its, write a number of body part words, according to the level you are teaching, e.g. *head, nose, ears, mouth, eyebrow, forehead, neck, shoulder, arm, elbow,* etc.

Ask a member of the class to be the 'model'. Then give each student a post-it note. They come to the front of the class and 'stick' the post-it on the correct body part on the student at the front.

Alternatively, draw a body shape on card (or you could ask a student to lie on some card and ask another student to draw around them so you have a real model) and use this to stick the post-its on.

## 2 Vocabulary: **Mime it!**

**Level:** Beginner to elementary.

**Preparation:** Make sure you have enough space for your students to walk around in the class. Bring in a set of the mini flashcards and some music, too.

**In class:** Ask students to walk around the room slowly to the music. Then ask one student to pick a card and say the injury. Students then mime the injury as they continue to walk (or limp) around the class.

*Example:*
**Students:** *Backache! We've got backache!*

**Variation:** For more advanced levels, put students into pairs. Give each pair one of the flashcards. They must create a mime to demonstrate the injury and to show how the player got his / her injury.

They then act these scenarios out in front of the class. The other students should guess the injury.

**Extension:** More advanced students can write up their football accident as part of a newspaper report. Give them the following model to help:

*Real Madrid superstar Cristiano Ronaldo was injured in the eighteenth minute. He was passing the ball when Liverpool's Steven Gerrard fouled him. Ronaldo fell and Gerrard stood on Ronaldo's foot. He was put on a stretcher and taken to hospital. He had an x-ray which showed the player has a broken left foot. Ronaldo will be out for three months.*

## 3 Speaking: **Doctor's waiting room**

**Level:** Intermediate to advanced.

**Preparation:** Photocopy and cut out enough mini flashcards for students to work in small groups. Arrange the chairs in your class as if in a doctor's waiting room.

**In class:** Put students into groups of three to five. Nominate one student to be a doctor, one a receptionist and the other students to be patients. The receptionist should give each patient a flashcard. The patients should not show this card to anyone. The patients should think or write about how they got their injury (it does not have to be football related). Remind students to use the past continuous and past simple.

The receptionist should call out the name of a patient who then sees the doctor. The doctor asks questions to find out how the injury happened and what the injury is.

*Example:*
**Doctor:** *What happened?*
**Patient:** *I was walking to school when I was hit by a car.*
**Doctor:** *Where does it hurt?*

## ④ Listening: True stories

**Level:** Intermediate.

**In class:** Here are four true stories about how players got their injuries. Read them to your students. They should make a note of:

- the player
- the injury
- what was happening just before the accident

1. *In 2000, French football star Thierry Henry was celebrating his goal against Chelsea. He ran to the corner. He ran straight into the corner post and hurt his face!*
2. *In 2003, David Beckham cut his head. But it wasn't on the pitch – it was in the dressing room. His former manager Sir Alex Ferguson was talking to the team. Sir Alex was angry and threw a football boot. It hit Beckham in the head!*
3. *The former England captain Bryan Robson was at the World Cup. He was in a hotel and he decided to play a joke on another player, Paul Gascoigne. Gascoigne was sleeping on his bed and Robson was trying to lift the bed to move it. But he dropped the bed on his foot and had to go home! He missed the World Cup!*
4. *Former England goalkeeper Dave Beasant was injured when he dropped a jar of salad cream. He was trying to stop the jar smashing onto the kitchen floor and it landed on his foot.*

**Extension:** Give students the stories and ask them to underline the past simple and the past continuous verb forms.
For homework, ask students to write about an injury that they (or a friend) experienced, using past simple and past continuous forms.

*Example:*
*Last year, I hurt my head. I was walking to school and I was writing a text on my phone when I walked into a lamp post.*

## Internet: Extra Time ▶

**Go to www.collinselt.com/football**

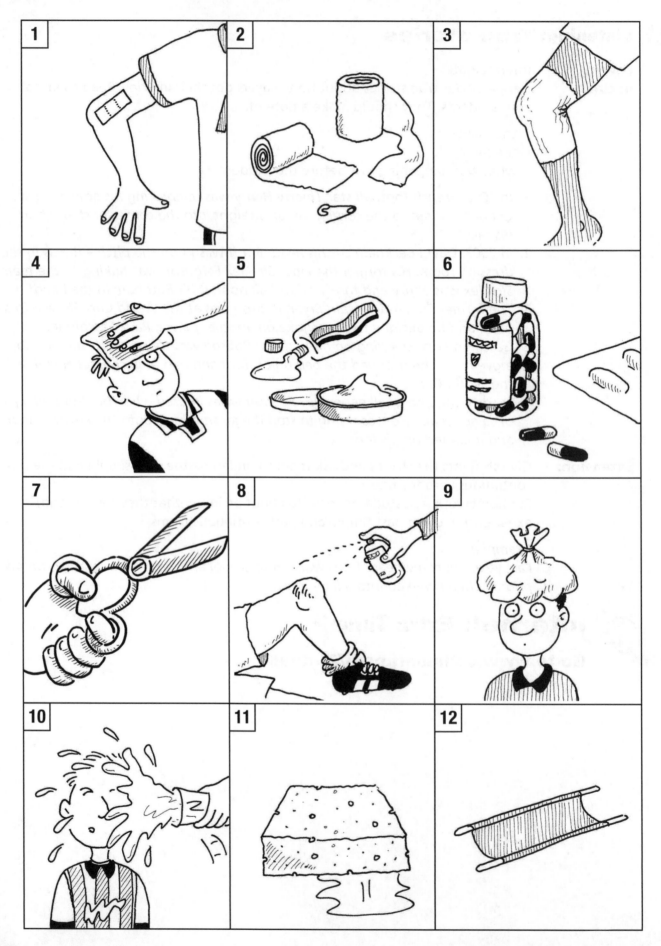

# Target Language

## First aid kit

1. a plaster
2. a bandage
3. an elastic / knee support
4. a compress
5. antiseptic cream
6. tablets / pills
7. scissors
8. analgesic spray
9. an ice pack
10. cold water
11. a sponge
12. a stretcher

## Football functions

## At the accident

- Call an ambulance / doctor / first aid.
- Call 999!
- Let's go to hospital / A & E. (Accident and Emergency)

## Talking to the patient

- Are you OK?
- Can you move your fingers / hand / arm / leg / toes?
- Do you feel sick?
- Do you feel dizzy?

## Advice

- Put on this plaster / bandage / cream / ice pack.
- Take these tablets / this medicine.
- You need an X-Ray.
- You need to rest.
- Have a glass of water.
- Take this tablet / pill / medicine …
  once a day / daily.
  twice / two / three times a day.
  with food / a drink.

# Using the pictures

## 1 Vocabulary: Presentation

| | |
|---|---|
| **Level:** | Elementary to intermediate. |
| **In class:** | Introduce the vocabulary using the mini flashcards. Ask concept questions as you present the new words: |

*Examples:*
- *Is anybody wearing a plaster? Why? What happened?*
- *When do you take a tablet?*
- *What other types of cream can you buy?* (e.g. hand cream, face cream, shaving cream, whipped cream)
- *Where do you normally see ice?* (e.g. in winter, in a fridge, in a cold drink etc.)

## 2 Vocabulary: Kim's game

| | |
|---|---|
| **Level:** | Beginner to intermediate. |
| **In class:** | Tell students that First-aiders always check their kit before they start work. Tell students you are going to put pictures of your first aid kit on the floor. They study the cards for 10 seconds. Then the students close their eyes. Remove a card. Ask students: *Which piece of my kit is not here?* |

Continue the game, but this time take away two cards, then take away three cards and so on.

## 3 Speaking and listening: Ambulance race

| | |
|---|---|
| **Level:** | Elementary to intermediate. |
| **Preparation:** | Photocopy the pictures and make mini flashcards, enough for your students to work in small teams. |
| **In class:** | Write '999' on the board and ask student what the number means. In the UK, this is the number you can call in an emergency. Ask your students what this number is in their country. |

Put your students into teams of three and give them a set of mini flashcards. Give each team a name (the English ambulance, super doctors, etc.). Then, students place the cards in front of them. Call out an injury. The team must find the correct card(s) for your injury and quickly bring it / them to you. They should say what you should do with the card.

*Example:*
**Teacher:** *Help! 999! I've cut my finger!*
**Student:** [*brings card 1*] *Put on this plaster!*

The team who arrives first with the correct suggestions gets a point. The team with the most points wins.

## 4 Speaking: Injury role-play

| | |
|---|---|
| **Level:** | Elementary to intermediate. |
| **Preparation:** | Prepare some flashcards for injuries from Unit 26, enough for half of your students |
| **In class:** | Divide your class into two teams. Team A are first-aiders, Team B are football players. The football players stand in a circle in the middle of the class, and the first-aiders stand outside the circle. Give the players a word card with an injury or illness on it. They should pretend to play football and mime this injury. |

The first-aiders should come into the circle and choose a player to treat. The first-aiders can ask questions.

*Example:*
*First-aider: Are you OK? Have you got a headache? Can you move your leg? Take these tablets. / Put on this plaster.*

Monitor the dialogues and feedback, writing any useful phrases or errors on the board. Then show another card. Then change over roles, so the first-aiders become the players.

**Variation:** This activity can be done in pairs, with the player picking a card and miming it and the first-aider diagnosing and testing the player.

## 5 Speaking and writing: Accident report form

**Level:** Intermediate.
**Preparation:** When there is an accident in a school, public place or office, an accident report form is filled in. Before the lesson, photocopy the accident report form below. Adjust the form according to your students' level.
**In class:** Divide your class into pairs, As and Bs. Ask both students to think of an accident they have had. Otherwise, they can invent an accident. Then they take it in turns to interview each other to complete the form.

---

**Accident Report Form**                                   Today's date: _____

Name of reporter: _____

Name of injured person: _____

Injury: _____          Date of accident: _____

Place of accident: _____

What happened? _____

_____

Treatment? _____

_____

Name of person who treated the injured person: _____

Hospital? Yes          No

Number of days off work / school because of injury: _____ days

Reporter's signature: _____

Injured person's signature: _____

---

## 6 Reading: First aid instructions

**Level:** Intermediate.
**Preparation:** Copy the instructions below to give out to students.
**In class:** Students read the instructions and match them to the flashcards from the unit.

1. *Shake well. Hold can 15cm from skin.*
2. *Clean area. Make sure skin is dry before you put on.*
3. *Take three times a day with liquid.*
4. *Clean the skin. Apply small amount to the skin. Wait two minutes before you apply a dressing.*

*Answers:* **1.** analgesic spray **2.** plaster **3.** tablet **4.** antiseptic cream

PHOTOCOPIABLE English Through Football 978-0-00-752234-7 www.collinselt.com/football

# Using the pictures

## 1 Vocabulary: **Mood mime**

| | |
|---|---|
| **Level:** | Beginner to intermediate. |
| **In class:** | Give a student one of the mini flashcards. The student leaves the classroom and enters miming the mood of the card. They should say, *I'm sorry I'm late!* in that mood. The rest of the class should guess the mood. |

## 2 Listening: **Who says it?**

| | |
|---|---|
| **Level:** | Elementary to intermediate. |
| **In class:** | Read the phrases below. Students match the phrases to the correct mini flashcard (suggested answers in brackets): |

1. *I don't believe it!* (card 5)
2. *It's boring! Let's go home.* (card 8 )
3. *I can't look!* (card 9 )
4. *They're a disgrace!* (card 3)
5. *We are the champions.* (card 7)
6. *What a result! Yes!* (card 4)

## 3 Listening: **Reactions**

| | |
|---|---|
| **Level:** | Elementary to intermediate. |
| **Preparation:** | Photocopy the pictures and make mini flashcards, enough for your students to work in small teams. |
| **In class:** | Write down or read out these eight football situations. Ask students to hold up or point to the correct mini flashcard and say how they feel in that situation. |

1. *Your striker scores a goal.*
2. *Your player misses a penalty.*
3. *Your captain gets injured.*
4. *Your striker scores a hat-trick.*
5. *Your goalkeeper lets in three goals.*
6. *There are no goals … and no action.*
7. *Your star player is sent off.*
8. *The other team's star player is sent off.*

*Example for 1:*
**Teacher:** *Your strikes scores a goal.*
**Student:** *[points to card 4] I feel happy.*

**Variation:** For more advanced students, give your students the situations in the present perfect:

1. *Your striker has just scored.*
2. *Your striker has just missed a penalty.*
3. *Your captain has just been injured.*
4. *Your striker has just scored a hat-trick.*
5. *Your goalkeeper has just let in three goals.*
6. *There have been no goals – and no action.*
7. *Your star player has just been sent off.*
8. *The other team's star player has been sent off.*

*Suggested answers:* **1.** (cards 4, 7) **2.** (cards 3, 6, 9) **3.** (cards 2, 9) **4.** (cards 4, 7) **5.** (cards 3, 6, 9) **6.** (card 8) **7.** (cards 3, 5, 6, 9) **8.** (cards 4, 7)

## ④ Speaking: How do you feel ...?

**Level:** Elementary to intermediate.
**Preparation:** Give this table to each of your students.
**In class:** Ask students, *How do you feel in these situations?*
*Tick ✔ the boxes that are true for you:*

| How do you feel ... | confident | worried | happy | bored | angry | disappointed |
|---|---|---|---|---|---|---|
| before an exam? | | | | | | |
| if you lose your mobile phone? | | | | | | |
| when you are going on a plane? | | | | | | |
| if you must wait in a queue? | | | | | | |
| when you find some money? | | | | | | |

Get class feedback and ask students to explain their choices. You can ask for more information, too.

*Examples:*
**Exams:** *How can you feel more confident before an exam?*
**Mobile phone loss:** *Where did you lose your phone? Did you find it again?*
**Air travel:** *How can you relax / take your mind off flying?*
**Queue:** *How do you feel if somebody pushes in front of you?*
**Money:** *What did you do with the money? Did you feel guilty?*

**Extension:** Ask students to think of another situation when they feel:
1. confident
2. nervous
3. angry
4. happy and excited

**114** Unit 28

## 5 Art and craft: **Mood draw**

**Level:** This task can be adapted to any level.

**Preparation:** Use the picture on Unit 41 and write numbers next to each blank face. Photocopy the page and give it to each student.

**In class:** Read out these sentences. (You can tailor your descriptions depending on the level of your students.)
Students listen and draw the appropriate expressions or actions.

1. *Fan number one is worried.*
2. *Fan number two is shocked.*
3. *Fan number three is angry.*
4. *Fan number four is bored.*
5. *Fans number five and six are happy.*

Students then swap drawings and guess what is happening.

***Example:*** *This crowd is bored. This game is boring. There are no goals!*

# Unit 29 Features of the Pitch

# Target Language

## Describing the pitch area

1. the pitch (U.S. English = the field)
2. the grass / turf
3. the touchline
4. the corner / corner flag
5. the goal
6. the net
7. the goal post
8. the bar / crossbar
9. the goal line
10. the centre circle
11. the penalty area
12. the penalty spot

## Extra vocabulary

- **the technical area:** This is the area between the pitch and the crowd. The manager and coach can stand here and give instructions to their players.
  *Example: Roy Hodgson is standing in the technical area.*
- **the bench:** This is where the substitutes sit.
- **the dug-out:** This is the area where the managers and other team members sit.
- **the wing / flank:** This is the area down the side of the pitch.
  *Example: Messi is running down the wing.*
- **the near / far post:** These are the goalposts closest to / furthest from where the ball is going.
  *Example: The ball has hit the near post!*

# Using the pictures

## 1 Vocabulary: Label the pitch

**Level:** Beginner to advanced.
**Preparation:** You will need a copy of Unit 42.
**In class:** Use the mini flashcards to elicit or pre-teach the words. Then give students the pitch outline (see Unit 42) for students to label. If you are teaching in a school with a football pitch, take your class outside and see if they can name the features that they see.

## 2 Vocabulary: Comprehension check

**Level:** Intermediate.
**Preparation:** Photocopy or copy on the board the sentences below.
**In class:** Give students these six sentences. Students circle the correct answer:

1. *He's trying to keep the ball in play, but it's over the **pitch**. / **touchline**.*
2. *The players are ready. They're coming out onto the **goal**. / **pitch**.*
3. *This pitch is terrible. The **pitch** / **grass** is too long!*
4. *The referee is pointing to the **goal post**. / **penalty spot**. It's a penalty to England!*
5. *And it's in the back of the **net**! / **penalty**! It's a goal to Italy!*
6. *That was close! The ball went over the **bar**. / **goal line**.*

*Answers:* **1.** touchline **2.** pitch **3.** grass **4.** penalty spot **5.** net **6.** bar

**Variation:** You can do this activity orally. Give pairs of students a set of the mini flashcards. They lay out these out on the table in front of them. Read out the sentences and students hold up the correct card.

## ③ Reading: **Dimensions test**

**Level:** Intermediate to advanced.

**Preparation:** This activity practises dimensions. You will need to bring in some rulers and / or a tape measure for the follow-up activity. Photocopy or copy on the board the gapped sentences below.

**In class:** Give students these dimensions of a standard international football pitch. They should choose the correct mini flashcard and fill the gap with the correct word.

1. *A _____ is 105 metres long and 68 metres wide.*
2. *The _____ is 11 metres away from the goal.*
3. *The _____ is 7.32 metres wide by 2.44 metres tall.*

*Answers:* **1.** pitch **2.** penalty spot **3.** goal

**Extension:** To follow up, ask students to find out these dimensions. Write the gapped prompts to help them if necessary:

1. *How big is our classroom? It's _____ long by _____ wide.*
2. *How wide is your desk? It's _____ wide.*
3. *How far is your home from school? It's _____ away from school.*

## ④ Vocabulary: **Shapes on the pitch**

**Level:** Elementary to advanced.

**Preparation:** Photocopy the pitch from Unit 42.

**In class:** Pre-teach these shapes, then ask students where they can be found on the football pitch (suggested answers in brackets).

- a square (in the goal net)

- a rectangle (the pitch shape, the penalty box, the ref's red and yellow cards)

- a circle (the centre circle, the penalty spot)

- a semi-circle (outside the penalty area; there is a quarter-circle near the corner flag)

- a triangle (the corner flag)

- a pentagon  (a football has 12 pentagons)

- a hexagon (a football has 20 hexagons)

**Extension:** Ask students to find these shapes in their classroom, in their homes, bags, purses, etc.

## 5 Vocabulary builder: **Sports venues**

**Level:**  Elementary to advanced.
**Preparation:**  Photocopy or copy on the board the table below.
**In class:**  Football is played on a pitch. But do your students know where these other sports are played? Students work in pairs and tick the correct boxes.

|  | pitch | court | track | course | ring | rink |
|---|---|---|---|---|---|---|
| football | | | | | | |
| basketball | | | | | | |
| golf | | | | | | |
| volleyball | | | | | | |
| rugby | | | | | | |
| cycling | | | | | | |
| boxing | | | | | | |
| tennis | | | | | | |
| horse race | | | | | | |
| ice-skating | | | | | | |
| athletics | | | | | | |

**Extension:**  Students should try and name as many famous venues, teams, or players for each of these sports as they can.
*Examples: Basketball: The LA Lakers play at the Staples Center and Luol Deng is a famous basketball player.*
*Golf: The Augusta golf course is a famous course and Rory McIlroy is a good golf player.*

## 6 Listening: **Hold up!**

**Level:**  Elementary to advanced.
**Preparation:**  Photocopy and cut out the mini flashcards, enough so your students can work in pairs. Then find a short, two-minute football match commentary. You can record one from the radio or use the Internet. Try **www.bbc.co.uk/radio** > *World Service* or *5 Live Sport* or check **www.collinselt.com**.
**In class:**  Put students into pairs. Place the mini flashcards face up on the table in front of them. Students listen to the football commentary. Every time they hear one of the features of the pitch mentioned, they should hold up the correct card.
Play the clip again, but press 'pause' each time you hear one of the features of the pitch in the commentary to check their answers.

# Unit 30  Things on the Pitch

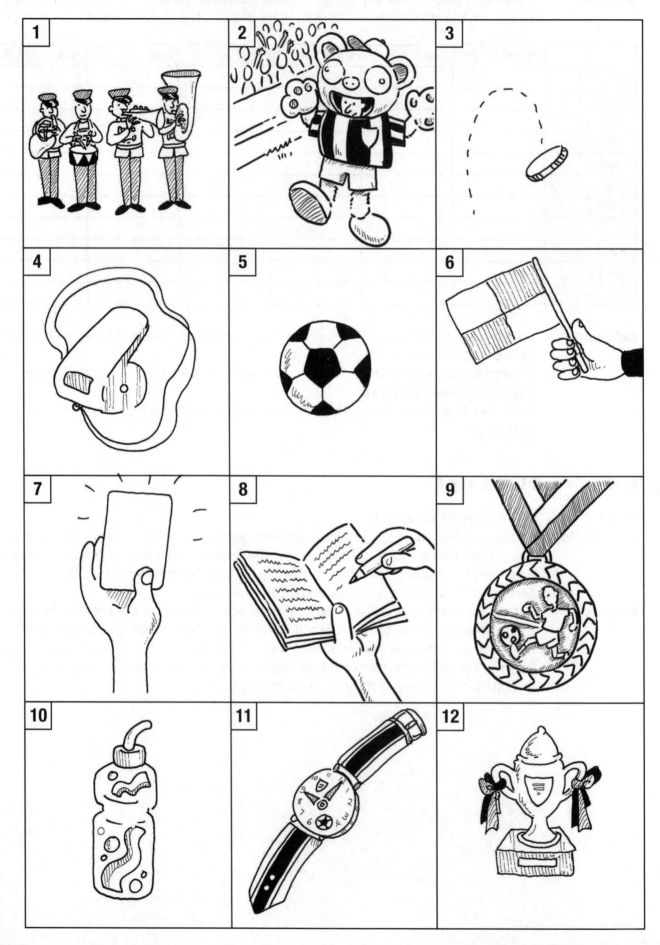

PHOTOCOPIABLE   English Through Football 978-0-00-752234-7   www.collinselt.com/football

# Target Language

## Things you see

1. a band
2. the mascot
3. a coin
4. the whistle
5. the ball
6. the assistant referee's / linesman's flag
7. a red / yellow card
8. the referee's notebook / book
9. a winner's medal
10. a drinks bottle
11. a watch
12. a cup / trophy

# Using the pictures

## ① Speaking: Questions

**Level:** Elementary to intermediate.

**In class:** As you teach the words using the mini flashcards, ask concept questions (suggested answers in brackets):

1. *What's the name of your favourite band? Can you play an instrument?*
2. *What's the mascot of your favourite sports team?*
3. *What's on the coins in your country? What's on the head – and the tail?*
4. *Who else uses a whistle?* (a policeman, sports teacher etc.)
5. *This is a football. What other types of ball are there?* (tennis ball, soft ball, rugby ball, basketball etc.)
6. *What are the colours of your national flag?*
7. *What happens when a player gets a red card?* (He gets sent off. He must leave the pitch.)
8. *When do you use a notebook? What do you write in it?*
9. *When do people get medals? Do you know anybody who has a medal? What did they get it for?*
10. *What do you drink after playing sport? What do you drink when you are cold / when you are at a party?*
11. *What colour / make is your watch? What time is it?*
12. *Do you know anyone who has a trophy? What did they get it for?*

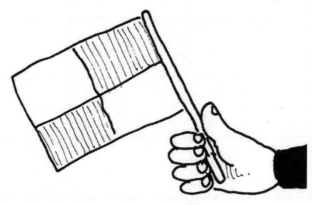

## 2 Listening: **Grab it!**

**Level:** Intermediate to advanced.

**In class:** Ask students to stand in a circle. Place the mini flashcards face-up on the floor, in the middle of the circle.

Read out these sentences to your students. Indicate the gap by making a noise or blowing a whistle. When your students know the missing word, they should grab the correct card from the floor and hold it up. The student with the most cards at the end wins. (Answers in brackets.)

1. *Before the match, the referee flips his _____. (coin)*
2. *The referee looks at his _____. Two minutes of extra time! (watch)*
3. *The referee is angry! He shows the player the _____ . (red card)*
4. *The referee blows his _____. It's the end of the match! (whistle)*
5. *The players are tired and thirsty. The coach throws them a _____ . (drink)*
6. *The _____ is made out of leather. (ball)*
7. *The referee is not happy with a player. He writes his name in his _____ . (notebook)*
8. *The _____ for the World Cup in South Africa was a leopard. (mascot)*
9. *That was offside! The assistant ref waves his _____. (flag)*
10. *And the captain holds the _____ . They are the winners of the World Cup! (trophy)*
11. *The _____ are playing the national anthem. (band)*
12. *The player collects his _____ from the Queen. She puts it around his neck. (medal)*

## 3 Vocabulary: **The objects game**

**Level:** This is an easy game suitable for all levels.

**Preparation:** Photocopy or copy on the board the table below.

**In class:** Put students into teams and give each team a copy of this table.

The teams must think of an object that would be found at that location. To make this more difficult, give students a letter – their object must start with the given letter.

When students have an item in the row for each category, they shout, *Referee! Game over!* Check the words and the spelling. If there are any mistakes, the game starts again until the team corrects their mistakes or another team gets the row.

| Letter | on the football pitch | in the classroom | at the hospital | at the station |
|--------|----------------------|------------------|-----------------|----------------|
| b |  |  |  |  |
| t |  |  |  |  |
| d |  |  |  |  |
| w |  |  |  |  |

Demonstrate what to do with one row before you start.
*Example:*

| Letter | on the football pitch | in the classroom | at the hospital | at the station |
|--------|----------------------|------------------|-----------------|----------------|
| b | ball | blackboard | beds | bags |

## ④ Writing: **Design a mascot**

**Level:**  Beginner to advanced.

**Preparation:**  Collect some examples of football mascots to show your class. See www.footballmascots.co.uk.

**In class:**  Show your students examples of football club mascots. Ask them if their club has a mascot. What is it? What is its name?

Now tell students to imagine their country is hosting the World Cup. What animal / object would they choose as a mascot? Why? Get them to discuss and then design their own mascot.

**Extension:**  For homework, students can write about their new mascot. Lower level students can use the following framework:

- *This is _____.*
- *He's / She's a _____.*
- *He's / She's a symbol of _____.*

## Internet: **Extra Time** ▶

**Go to www.collinselt.com/football**

# Unit 31  The Game

# Target Language

## Describing a match

1. to kick-off / the kick off
2. half-time
3. full-time
4. a goal
5. a penalty
6. an own goal
7. the score
8. to win / a win
9. to lose / a defeat
10. to draw / a draw
11. injury time
12. a penalty shoot-out / sudden death

## Extra vocabulary

- extra time, stoppage time
- a match day
- a home match (= in your stadium)
- an away match (= in your opponent's stadium)
- a league
- to be champions / to finish top of the league
- to be promoted (= to go up a league)
- to be relegated / demoted (= to go down a league)

# Using the pictures

## 1 Reading: Complete a report

**Level:** Intermediate.
**Preparation:** Photocopy or copy on the board the gapped report below.
**In class:** Give groups of students a set of mini flashcards each. Give students the match report. Students write the number of the correct card in the correct place. (Answers below.)

1. _____ was at three o'clock. The first half was quiet and slow. But then Wayne Rooney scored a 2. _____ in 43 minutes – just two minutes before 3. _____.

After 4. _____, everything changed. Germany came back at England. England defender John Terry kicked Lukas Podolski. The referee gave Germany a 5. _____. Podolski scored.
It was bad luck for England in the 85th minute, just before 6. _____ when Gerrard hurt his knee. The referee added on three minutes of 7. _____.

In the 93rd minute, there were more problems for England. Defender Rio Ferdinand passed the ball back to Robert Green, but the England goalkeeper did not see it, and the ball went into the net. It was an 8. _____. 2-1 to Germany. It was 9. _____ for Germany and 10. _____for England!

*Answers:* **1.** card 1, kick off **2.** card 4, goal **3.** card 2, half time **4.** card 2, half time **5.** card 5, penalty **6.** card 3, full time **7.** card 11, injury time **8.** card 6, own goal **9.** card 8, a win **10.** card 9, a defeat

**Variation:** Read out the match report. Ask students to hold up the correct cards. Then see if your students can retell the story of the match, using the cards as a guide.

## 2 Grammar: A football story

**Level:** Elementary to advanced.
**In class:** Divide students into pairs and give them a set of mini flashcards each. They can use the cards to invent their own football match story, putting the cards into any order.
Pre-teach the following linking words and phrases (appropriate to their level). They should then tell their story to the class.

> **Linking phrases**
>
> **Sequence:**
> *firstly, later, then, after that, next*
>
> **Contrast:**
> *but, however, on the other hand*
>
> **Result:**
> *so, because of this, therefore, as a result, as a consequence*

# ③ Writing: My match report

**Level:**        Elementary to intermediate.
**Preparation:** Photocopy or copy on the board the model report below.
**In class:**     Ask students to watch or think of a recent football match.
              Students write a post-match report. They can use the framework below as a model.

**Match:** _____ v. _____
**Date:** _____

- The kick-off was at _____.

- At half-time, the score was _____.

- In the second half, _____ scored a goal.

- _____ scored an own goal.

- There were_____ minutes of injury time.

- At full time, the score was _____.

- There was a / no penalty shoot-out.

- _____ won the penalty shoot-out.

**My verdict:**
- It was a fair / unfair result.
- The man of the match was _____.
- This match was exciting / nerve-racking / forgettable / boring.

# Target Language

## Describing actions

1. to pass the ball (a short pass)
2. to pass the ball (a long pass)
3. to dribble the ball
4. to shoot / take a shot
5. to head the ball (a header)
6. to take a free kick
7. to take a throw-in
8. to take a goal kick
9. to take a corner

## Extra vocabulary

- to warm up
- to save / a save
- to score (a goal)
- to score a hat-trick (= three goals in one match)
- to volley
- to take / score / miss a penalty
- to handle the ball

## Football verbs: Advanced skills

- **to do an overhead / scissors / bicycle kick:** To kick the ball at head height over your body and away from the direction you are playing. *Example: Rooney did an amazing overhead kick in the tenth minute.*
- **to dummy / a dummy:** To fool another player. *Example: It was a beautiful dummy by Fabregas – he sent the goalie the wrong way.*
- **to nutmeg / a nutmeg:** When a player puts the ball through another player's legs. *Example: And he nutmegged the goalkeeper!*
- **to bend the ball:** To kick the ball in a way that it changes direction in the air. *Example: Not many players can bend the ball like David Beckham can.*
- **to showboat / showboating:** When a player 'shows off' their skill during a match. *Example: That was a bit of showboating by Ronaldo.*

# Using the pictures

## 1 Vocabulary: Mime it!

**Level:** Elementary to intermediate.

**In class:** Put your students into pairs. Each pair should pick a mini flashcard at random and then mime the action on it to their partner, who should guess the action.

*Example for lower levels:*
**Student A:** *Are you passing the ball?*
**Student B:** *Yes, I am.*

*Example for more advanced levels:*
**Student A:** *Are you bending the ball round the wall?*
**Student B:** *Yes, I am, and I've scored a goal!*

## 2 Speaking and listening: Move it!

**Level:** Elementary to advanced.

**Preparation:** Photocopy the pitch outline (see Unit 42) and the mini flashcards enough times so your students can work in pairs. Bring in counters (to represent players) and a mini ball / marble for each pair.

**In class:** Student A should pick out three cards and not show them to his / her partner. Student A places the cards in an order that shows some moves in a football match. S/he should describe the moves. Student B must move the counters and ball across the pitch accordingly.

*Example:*
**Student A:** *He takes a corner. The striker heads the ball. The goalie saves.*

## 3 Grammar: Class football awards

**Level:** Elementary to advanced.

**Preparation:** Prepare a list of your national team's players, or the most famous players in your country and write their names on the board. Alternatively, if you have a school team, you can write the school player names on the board. Also copy the list of questions below.

**In class:** Tell your students that every year, there are a number of football awards such as Fifa's World Player of the Year. Give your students the questions below. They match the questions to the correct mini flashcard.
Divide your students into groups of three or four. Students should discuss their answers. Then feedback as a class, voting on a winner for each category and an overall winner. You can award the winning player a trophy (see Unit 39 for a cup outline).

1. *Who is the best at heading the ball?*
2. *Who is the best at passing the ball?*
3. *Who is the best at dribbling?*
4. *Who is the best at taking free kicks?*
5. *Who is the best at taking corners?*
6. *Who is the best at taking goal kicks?*
7. *Who is the best at doing long passes?*
8. *Who is the best at shooting?*
9. *Who is the best at taking throw-ins?*

**Variation:** Give more advanced students different superlative forms.

*Example:*
*Who is the best at taking corners? Who is the fastest at dribbling? Who is the most accurate at taking free kicks?*

**Extension:** If you have younger learners, give them a copy of The World Cup from Unit 39. Ask them to colour the trophy in class or for homework.

**Internet: Extra Time ▶**

Go to **www.collinselt.com/football**

# Target Language

## Describing fouls

1. to kick
2. to trip
3. to stamp on
4. to charge into / barge
5. to push / shove
6. to hit
7. to hold someone back / pull someone's shirt
8. to push someone off the ball
9. to touch / handle the ball (= handball)

## Extra vocabulary: Referee's actions

- to book a player
- to show a player a yellow / red card
- to send someone off

## Players

- to foul someone / to commit a foul
- the player was booked
- the player was shown a yellow / red card
- the player was sent off
- to be a 'dirty' player

## Football phrases: Manager and fans

- The manager is protesting / the fans are complaining.
- The fans are angry / furious.
- It was a good / fair decision.
- It was a bad / an unfair decision.
- The ref made some good / bad decisions.

# Using the pictures

## 1 Vocabulary: Lead-in

**Level:** Beginner to advanced.

**In class:** Put students into small groups. Show them one of the mini flashcards, then get them to think of other examples of bad behaviour or cheating in football. Elicit / Present the words in English and use the flashcards to drill the words. How many of the fouls did your students already know?

## 2 Grammar: **Football rules**

**Level:**       Elementary to advanced.

**In class:**   Students use the cards to make a list of football rules. Ask them what you must / mustn't do or are not allowed to do / have to do.

*Examples:*
*You mustn't pull another player's shirt.*
*You must play with 11 men.*
*You must wear football boots.*
*You mustn't touch the ball.*

**Extension:**  Put students into pairs and give them these other places and situations. Give them two minutes to think of as many rules for each one as they can.

**1.** *in class*
**2.** *driving on the street*
**3.** *at the swimming pool*
**4.** *on a plane / at an airport*
**5.** *in an exam*
**6.** *in a game of basketball*

## 3 Writing: **New rules**

**Level:**       Elementary to advanced.

**In class:**   Students write a new rule for football that they would like to introduce. Depending on their level, students should use one or all of the following: *can / can't; must / mustn't; allowed to / not allowed to.*

*Examples:*
• *Players can't argue with the referee.*
• *Players must shake hands with each other after the game.*
• *Players must give some of their salary to charity.*
• *Players are allowed to take off their shirts when they celebrate.*

**Extension:**  Ask students to think of a new rule they would like to introduce for these places:

**1.** *at school / in class*
**2.** *on a bus / train*
**3.** *in a cinema*
**4.** *in a supermarket*
**5.** *on the Internet*

## 4 Speaking: **Consequences**

**Level:**         Intermediate.

**Preparation:**  This game revises past tenses. Bring in some coins.

**In class:**     Put students into pairs. Place the mini flashcards face down and give each pair a coin. Tell students that one side of the coin is 'just before' and the other side is 'just after'.
Student A flips the coin. Student B turns over a card. They must make a sentence saying what happened just before or just after the action on the card.

*Example:*
**Student A:** [*flips coin which shows 'just before'*] *Just before.*
**Student B:** [*turns over card 7*] *The striker was running into the box – he was close to the goal so the defender pulled his shirt.*
**Student A:** [*flips coin which shows 'just after'*] *Just after.*
**Student B:** [*turns over card 1*] *The referee didn't see the foul. The striker and the fans were furious.*

## 5 Writing and speaking: Red card rules

**Level:** This can be used at any level.

**Preparation:** The cards used by the referee can be used as a rules / rewards system for your class. You will need to make red and yellow cards for this. You can use the templates from Unit 43.

**In class:** Use the red / yellow cards to show students different types of grammatical or written error. Use the yellow cards for content errors or improvements and use the red cards to show an unacceptable howler – an easy mistake that they should know for their level. You could write their errors on red / yellow cards and place them on the board for the class to correct as a group. If they can correct the error, remove it from the card.

**Variation:** Use this for younger learners. Show your students the red and yellow cards. Explain to your students that, like in football, the yellow card is a warning card and a red card is a consequence card. Decide and clarify what a red card offence is – it could be for not handing in homework, it could be swearing, it could be for being late. Students get a yellow card as a warning and their name is written on the card. For a serious or repeated offence you move them to the red card. This means the consequence will be a discussion with the head teacher / parents (in accordance with your school behaviour policy).

## Internet: Extra Time ▶

**Go to www.collinselt.com/football**

# Unit 34  Dream Team

# Target Language

## Defence / The defenders

1. the goalkeeper (goalie)
2. the right back / wing back
3. the left back / centre half
4. the centre back / centre half
5. the centre back / wing back

## Midfield / The midfielders

6. the central midfielder / holding midfielder
7. the right side of midfleld
8. the left side of midfield

## Attack / The attackers

9. the striker / centre forward
10. on the left wing / the left winger
11. on the right wing / the right winger

## Extra vocabulary: The people

- a team  (11 players)
- a squad
- the manager
- the coach
- the substitutes

- to be substituted
- to be on the bench
- a right-footed player
- a left-footed player

## Formations

- **4-4-2:** four defenders, four midfielders and two strikers
- **5-3-2:** five defenders, three midfielders and two strikers
- **4-5-1:** four defenders, five midfielders and one striker
- **4-3-3:** four defenders, three midfielders and three strikers

# Using the pictures

## 1 Vocabulary: Name the team

**Level:** Beginner to advanced.

**In class:** Go over the target language with the class. Ask students to identify the formation of the team on page 136 (it is 4-3-3). Now ask students to think of the players in their favourite or national team. They can write the players' names on the team picture (page 136).

When they have finished, students can compare teams. If they have different teams, which team do they think is the best?

## ② Vocabulary: **Starting positions**

**Level:** Beginner to advanced.

**Preparation:** Write the position words on the card templates (see Unit 43): *goalkeeper*, *striker*, etc. Stick the cards in the corners of the classroom.

**In class:** After you have taught the vocabulary, check comprehension by playing this game. Find out the positions of a number of famous football players that your students know.

Students stand in the middle of the class. Call out a footballer's name. Students run and stand in the corner of the room by the position they think this person plays in.

*Example:*
- *Patrice Evra (defender)*
- *Lionel Messi (striker)*
- *Cassillas (goalkeeper)*
- *Cristiano Ronaldo (striker)*
- *Fabregas (midfielder)*
- *Ribery (left winger)*

## ③ Writing: **My team**

**Level:** This task can be adapted for any level.

**In class:** Ask students to name the players in their school team, their national team or the most popular teams in the class.

Students write about a team. They describe the players using the target language.

*Example:*
*In the German national team, there are two strikers. There is Miroslav Klose and Mario Gomez. Gomez is right-footed… etc.*

## ④ Writing and speaking: **My dream team**

**Level:** This task can be adapted for any level.

**Preparation:** Prepare a list of football players who are in your country's league, international league or in an international tournament. You can check on **www.fifa.com** for world tournaments, **www.uefa.com** for a European tournaments and **www.premierleague.com** for the English Premier League.

**In class:** Tell students they are managers of a dream team. They can give their team a name and design a badge and kit. They can use the outlines in Units 36 and 37 for this. Students choose eleven real players for their team. Give them a list of players to help. Make sure students have the right number of strikers, midfielders, defenders and a goalkeeper. They should write about their team. You can supply one of these language models, depending on the students' level of English.

*Example for beginner to elementary level:*
*This is my team. Its name is …*
*I'm the manager and my name is …*
*In my team, I've got …*

*Example for pre-intermediate level:*
*I'm … and I'm the manager of a new team for … (country / city). Its name is …*
*This is our badge.*
*I've bought eleven new players. In goal I've got … because he is …*

*Example for upper intermediate to advanced levels:*
*Welcome to the richest club in the world.*
*I'm the new manager of the brand new super-club called …*
*Here is our badge / emblem, which depicts …*
*And now the most important part of the press conference. I will unveil our new players. First, you'll be watching … He is a … striker with …*

**Variation:** Younger learners can draw the players (or find photos from magazines or the Internet) to put with their descriptions.

## ⑤ Reading: **Dream team manager**

**Level:** This is an ongoing activity for any level, which can last one week or for a whole football tournament. It encourages students to analyse match data in English.

**In class:** You can play this game before a tournament or before a certain number of league games. Ask students to pick a dream team with a variety of players from different teams in it. Collect in the dream teams and display them on the walls. After a match, students need to check how their dream team players did. They can do this by checking the football pages of a newspaper or looking online. Students get points as follows, depending on how their players performed:

| Dream Team Manager: Points System | |
|---|---|
| **Action** | **Points** |
| • Their dream team player plays in the match: | + add one point per player |
| • Their dream team strikers score a goal: | + two points per goal |
| • Their midfield players score a goal: | + three points per goal |
| • Their defenders score a goal: | + five points per goal |
| • Their goalie lets in a goal: | -1 point per goal |
| • A dream team player gets a yellow card: | -2 points per card |
| • A dream player gets a red card: | -4 points per card |

At the end of the agreed number of matches, students add up all of their points. Who is the top manager in your class? You can award them the trophy from Unit 39 as a reward.

# Unit 35  A Football

PHOTOCOPIABLE   **English Through Football** 978-0-00-752234-7   www.collinselt.com/football

# Unit 36  Football Emblem

# Unit 37  Football Kit

# Unit 38  Football Kit: Beetle Game

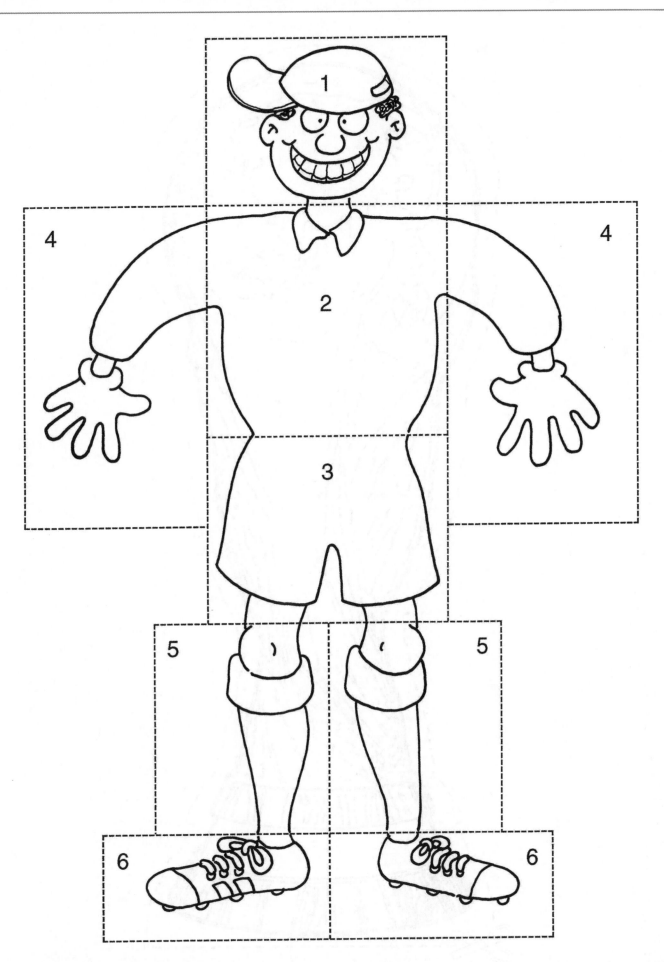

# Unit 39 The World Cup

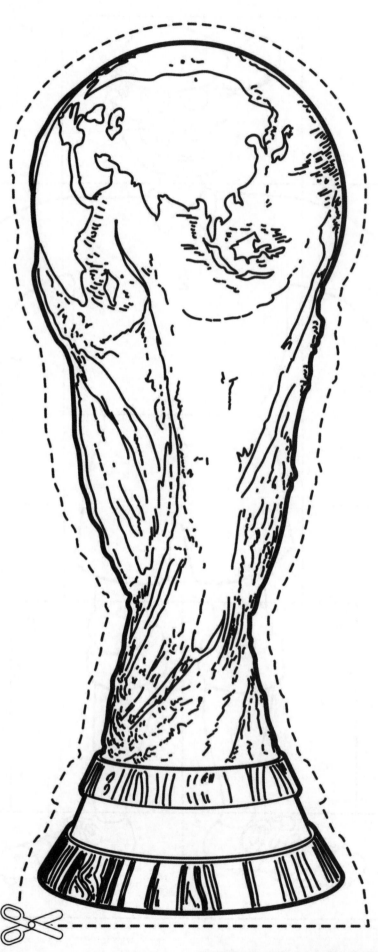

# Unit 40  Tickets to the Match

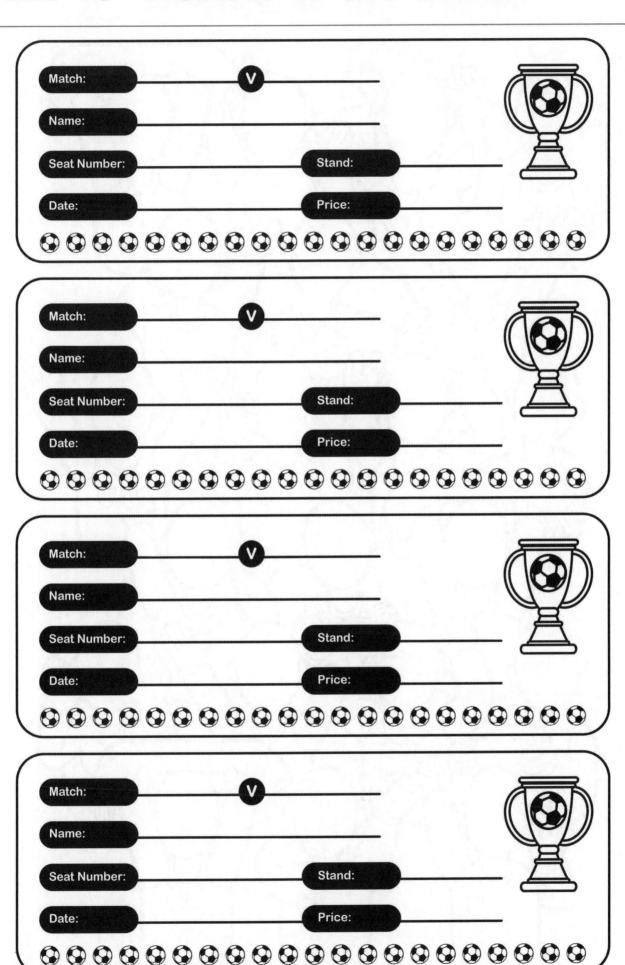

Match: _____ V _____

Name: _____

Seat Number: _____  Stand: _____

Date: _____  Price: _____

Match: _____ V _____

Name: _____

Seat Number: _____  Stand: _____

Date: _____  Price: _____

Match: _____ V _____

Name: _____

Seat Number: _____  Stand: _____

Date: _____  Price: _____

Match: _____ V _____

Name: _____

Seat Number: _____  Stand: _____

Date: _____  Price: _____

# Unit 42  Pitch Outline

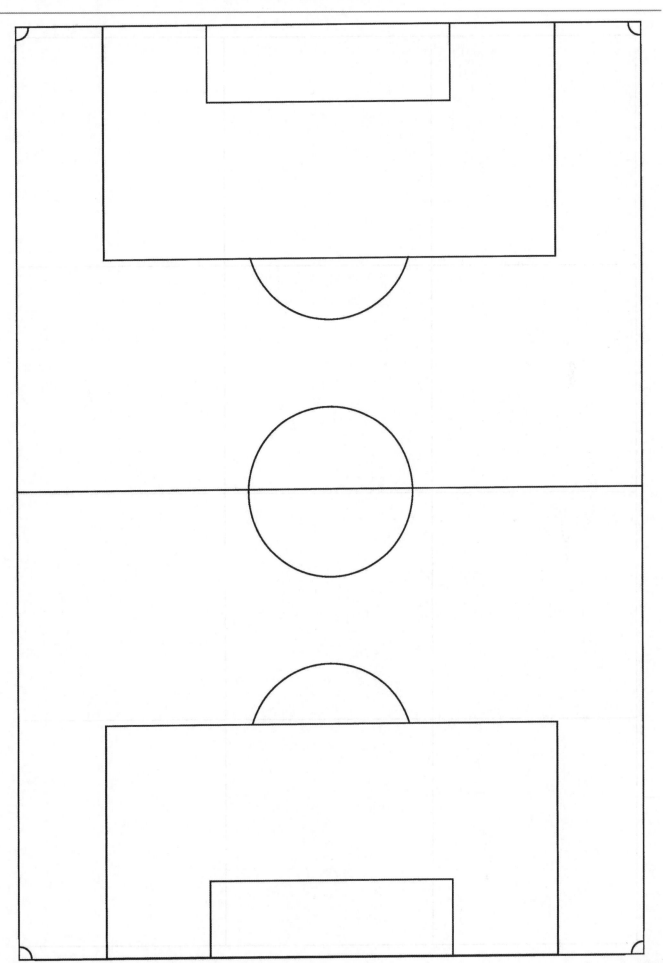

# Unit 43  Card Template

# Also available from Collins:

## Mini Flashcards Language Games

Nineteen packs of 40 full-colour flashcards with games and suggested activities, for learners to use in class. Suitable for all ages and levels.

978-0-00-752236-1

978-0-00-752237-8

978-0-00-752238-5

978-0-00-752239-2

978-0-00-752240-8

978-0-00-752241-5

978-0-00-752242-2

978-0-00-752243-9

978-0-00-752244-6

www.collinselt.com

978-0-00-752245-3

978-0-00-752246-0

Mini Flashcards
Language Games

Prepositions
& Directions

Collins

978-0-00-752247-7

978-0-00-752248-4

978-0-00-752249-1

978-0-00-752250-7

978-0-00-752251-4

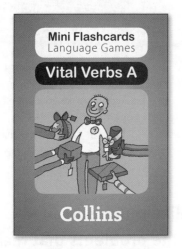

978-0-00-752253-8

978-0-00-752269-9

978-0-00-752268-2

www.collinselt.com

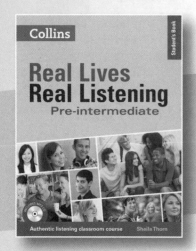 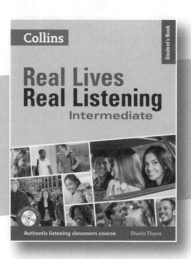 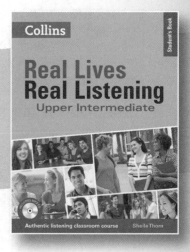
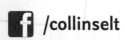
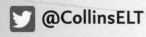